Contents

Introduction

CASTLE GARDEN

WONDERS OF MAN

STATUE
OF LIBERTY

by Oscar Handlin

and the Editors
of the Newsweek Book Division

NEWSWEEK, New York

NEWSWEEK BOOK DIVISION

JOSEPH L. GARDNER   *Editor*

Janet Czarnetzki   *Art Director*
Edwin D. Bayrd, Jr.   *Associate Editor*
Laurie P. Phillips   *Picture Editor*
Eva Galan   *Assistant Editor*
Lynne H. Brown   *Copy Editor*
Russell Ash   *European Correspondent*

S. ARTHUR DEMBNER   *Publisher*

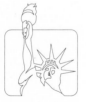

WONDERS OF MAN

MILTON GENDEL   *Consulting Editor*

Conceived as a monument to Franco-American friendship, to be erected on the centennial of the Declaration of Independence, the Statue of Liberty has come to stand for a good deal more. Only a fraction of the one million who visit Liberty Island each year know the gigantic statue's official name, *Liberty Enlightening the World*. Yet most of them can recite the final lines of Emma Lazarus's poem about it: "Give me your tired, your poor . . ."

Immigration to the United States increased at an impressive and almost steady rate throughout the nineteenth century. But 1886, the date the statue was finally unveiled in New York harbor, was not a peak year — only 334,203 immigrant aliens arrived at the thresholds of America. Almost immediately thereafter, however, the numbers swelled, to reach an average of 982,655 for each of the twelve years following 1903. World War I stemmed the tide sweeping across the Atlantic from Europe and, except for three years in the 1920's, the annual figure never again exceeded a half million. A restrictive immigration law passed in 1924 closed the golden door to many, while the depression decade of the 1930's made America seem a less desirable haven.

Still the Statue of Liberty has remained a noble if no longer always valid symbol of a United States offering its incomparable liberties — religious and political liberty, as well as freedom from want and fear — to all mankind. It is this aspect of the statue that the distinguished scholar who has written the following narrative chooses to emphasize. Serving as a vivid counterpoint to his text are haunting photographs of immigrants and impressionistic views of the statue and nearby Ellis Island today. Taken together, the text and illustrations offer a new insight into a story that continues to have meaning for each new generation of Americans.

THE EDITORS

LADY WITH A LAMP: SYMBOL OF LIBERTY

I

A GIFT FROM THE OLD WORLD

On June 21, 1871, the steamer *Pereire* of the Compagnie Transatlantique entered New York harbor after a crossing of thirteen days. The vessel dropped anchor in the bay while waiting to clear quarantine. The weather was fine. A young French passenger noted with delight the wide expanse of the harbor and the swift movement of innumerable ships along its waters. He observed with special interest those immense steam vessels called ferryboats, very much like floating houses. Two stories high, the center reserved for vehicles, they darted across the bay in all directions. Full of people and covered with flags, they occasionally made their presence known by shrieking whistles. He found something impressive, as Walt Whitman also did, in the sight of thousands of people drawn together for the crossing, then hastening away, each to his own appointed task.

In the background, across the trail left by little sailboats, the new arrival made out the slopes of Jersey City on the left and of Brooklyn on the right, and between them, New York. The three municipalities seemed parts of one city, and he immediately perceived the monumental possibilities of Bedloe's Island, which lay at the center of the upper bay, square in the field of vision of any newcomer to America's greatest city.

In town, the noise and bustle of the streets overwhelmed the visitor. Omnibuses, heavily loaded trucks, and a variety of other vehicles clogged the neglected roadways. A web of wires dangling from the awkward telegraph poles added to the impression of disorder. The garish signs, awnings, and shutters of the shops, the merchandise exposed on the sidewalks, the hawkers along the way, all gave the stranger a sense of undis-

Lower Broadway in the 1870's

ciplined individualism. Much was odd to a man brought up in Paris — a building of eight stories next to a neighbor of two, occasional trees jutting without design from the pavement, and architecture that could only be defined as Anglo-Marseillaise-Gothic-Doric-Chinese. But most difficult of all to understand, he wrote in a letter shortly after landing, was the character of the Americans — so similar to that of Europeans, yet so different, so national, yet so complex and varied. In a long journey across the whole continent he would seek answers to the questions that troubled him.

The passenger who disembarked from the *Pereire* that June day had not arrived out of the tourist's idle curiosity. He had come on a mission with a deep personal meaning.

Frédéric Auguste Bartholdi had been born on August 2, 1834, in Colmar, a thriving little city in lower Alsace. His family was probably Italian in origin, but had settled generations earlier in the Swiss canton of Thurgau. In the seventeenth century one branch had moved down the Rhine through Germany and had finally come to rest in Alsace. The Bartholdis had long been Protestants and had traditionally valued schooling. Education gave them a prominent place in the life of the region. Among Frédéric Auguste's ancestors were several notable pastors, and also prominent physicians, pharmacists, and lawyers. His father was a well-known burgher and officeholder, and his mother, Charlotte Beysser, came from an equally reputable and solid line. Their circumstances were comfortable. Auguste, as he was called, could look forward to a placid upbringing.

Tragedy, however, struck the family with the death of the father in 1836, when Auguste had just passed his second birthday. Charlotte, a redoubtable woman — tall, dignified, and powerful — thereafter concentrated her energies on her two sons. She moved to Paris, partly in order to take care of some property interests there, mostly to supervise better the education of her children. The ties to Colmar nevertheless remained strong, fortified by regular visits to the ancestral home she still owned and by numerous friendships in the vicinity.

The links to Alsace undoubtedly helped give Bartholdi his start in life. He had been a desultory student, working his way without distinction through the Lycée Louis-le-Grand, until he discovered an interest in art. In Colmar on vacation he had his first formal art lessons and back in Paris he found a place in the atelier of the painter Ary Scheffer. Early on, Auguste decided that his true medium was sculpture and shifted his efforts to the studio of the well-known sculptor Jean François Soitoux. He also took some instruction in architecture at that time with Eugène Emmanuel Viollet-le-Duc.

Bartholdi thus had the best training the times afforded, and his teachers approved of the work and the diligence of the likable young man. But it took more than that to secure the commissions that made sculpture — and especially monumental sculpture — possible.

Such an artist required commissions. A painter, by contrast, could turn out landscapes and historical or genre pictures as inspiration moved him, set them in frames, and wait for a purchaser. It did not matter on what wall his oils or watercolors hung. Marble and bronze, however, were more expensive than canvas and colors, and the sculptor as he worked needed some

A contemporary Currier and Ives print captures bustling New York harbor as it appeared when Auguste Bartholdi dis-

embarked in 1871. Bedloe's Island, future site of the Statue of Liberty, lies beyond the cylindrical bulk of Castle Garden.

vision of where the statue would finally stand, for much of its appearance depended upon its setting. He could not simply produce figures for his own attic and wait for future recognition. Often the first step in creation was contact with the potential purchaser.

The patrons of the past were no longer in the market, however. The princes who had used their wealth to embellish churches, squares, tombs, and palaces were not, in the nineteenth century, making the displays of generosity that they had before the French Revolution. A few individuals wished still to have their portraits perpetuated in marble busts; and Bartholdi would ultimately get his share of such petty business. But the great works, in size and in opportunity for the stretch of the imagination, now generally found support in commissions from government. The state wished thus to honor its heroes, and the municipalities, to display their civic virtues; only they commanded both the space and the funds.

It took diplomacy as well as artistic genius to do well in these affairs. The cautious politicians who made the decisions and disbursed the money required delicate handling to yield to the necessity of paying for what they could not see in advance. The sketch on paper or even the plaster model submitted in a competition rarely gave an adequate impression of the finished product; and every taxpayer knew what he liked, even if he did not know how to explain what or why. Once the grant was made, there still remained negotiations — over costs, over suggested modifications of the original design, and over complaints about unforeseen details — and the settlement often stretched out for years. Even after he was well established, Bar-

tholdi would have plenty of heartaches, including a long-drawn-out lawsuit against the city of Marseilles. For a youth seeking a start, the problem of the first commission was imposing.

In this respect the Colmar connection proved useful. The town prospered and, as it spread out, acquired both space and funds. Its residents, living in a cultural borderland, had a conscious desire to make their own identity known. They were French and intensely patriotic, yet their language was a German dialect. They were therefore very aware of their uniqueness and they wished to preserve it. One way of doing so was to commemorate native heroes. And another was to employ local artists for the purpose.

Bartholdi's opportunity came when the city fathers decided to erect a monument in honor of General Jean Rapp, a Colmar boy who had gone on to become one of Napoleon's marshals. The commission went to Auguste, then just about eighteen years old. No doubt it would be cheaper that way; and family ties and local pride also helped. The monument, unveiled in 1856 when Bartholdi was twenty-two, immediately made his reputation.

Success, of course, was not earned in a day. In time, Bartholdi would have the Legion of Honor, songs composed to express the gratitude of Colmar, and promises of love and immortality. But his project for a monument to Admiral Armand Joseph Bruat, first proposed in 1855, was not built until 1864; and his plan for a monumental tower for Marseilles never left the drawing board. Still he had no dearth of assignments — a fountain in Bordeaux, a statue of Vauban in Avallon, and one of Vercingetorix in Clermont-Ferrand.

Nattily attired and clean-shaven, Auguste Bartholdi strikes a calculatedly romantic pose — one that reflects both the solemnity and the vision of Liberty's creator. The Frenchman's masterwork, conceived in Suez in 1856, when the sculptor was only twenty-two, was finally erected some 8,000 miles away in 1886. By that time the central concept had been altered and only the figure itself — a toga-clad woman holding a torch — survived.

Nevertheless, growing fame did not satisfy the artist's desire for another kind of achievement. In 1856 he had made a trip through Egypt with Auguste Nefftzer, a journalist friend. Bartholdi had admired the great ancient sculptures which outlived the past, transcended the present, and reached toward the infinite future. The simple surfaces, marked off by clear forceful lines, persuaded him that all true art expressed the power of an idea. Once the idea infused the creator, the work rose by itself, surmounting all the limitations of material and execution.

Thereafter Auguste was on the lookout for the inspiring idea. At Suez he thought he had it: the West handing civilization on to the East — in accord with the expansion of Europe in the second half of the nineteenth century. Visually his imagination saw a lighthouse at Suez, in the form of a beautiful woman, draped in an antique robe, her right arm holding up a torch. Nothing came of it. The quest for an idea continued.

In 1870, a year before his arrival in New York, reality broke in upon the life of the thirty-six-year-old sculptor. The outbreak of the war with Prussia stirred his emotions; patriotic and military themes had been prominent in his own works and Alsatians were particularly sensitive to relations with Germany. The loss of the province to the new German empire as a result of defeat was to be a humiliating blow.

Personal chagrin deepened Bartholdi's dismay at the course of events. At the outbreak of hostilities in July 1870 he had secured a commission in the National Guard. He was after all unmarried, had no objection to wearing a smart uniform, and did not conceive that his

Although the widow Bartholdi left Colmar for Paris when her son was only two years old, Auguste maintained an intense devotion to his native Alsace throughout his life. His loyalty is reflected in three monuments situated in or near Colmar. The earliest and least imposing of these is Bartholdi's 1856 statue of Jean Rapp (right), the Colmar boy who became one of Napoleon's marshals, served with distinction in Russia, rallied to the deposed emperor's side during the Hundred Days, and was briefly exiled for his unswerving devotion. The largest is a 38-foot-high granite lion (above), dedicated to the defenders of nearby Belfort. That Alsatian community, which commands a strategic pass in the Jura Mountains, had held off a German siege force throughout the Franco-Prussian War and was the only part of Alsace not ceded to Bismarck in 1871. Bartholdi's bizarre tribute to the combat dead of that war, a cenotaph in the form of a desecrated tomb (opposite), is a grim reminder of the high cost of high diplomacy.

AU GENERAL RAPP

involvement would be serious. In August he arranged a transfer from Paris to Colmar to be near his mother. Thus it happened that he was in charge — no one else was around — when the enemy advanced to the bridge over the Rhine at the nearby town of Horbourg. Fiasco. Auguste rounded up fifteen men, went down the road, heard that the Germans were five thousand strong, and turned around. With no resistance Colmar fell, leaving Bartholdi with bitter reflections. His decision had been practical. Had it been heroic?

Meanwhile Napoleon III had abdicated, and France slid hesitantly toward republican status. Then that doughty old warrior on behalf of liberal causes Giuseppe Garibaldi arrived uninvited from Italy to take a hand. The nervous French provisional government, unsure of its own intentions as well as of those of the swashbuckling old man, desired mostly to keep him harmless and at a distance. Bartholdi's final military experience was as liaison officer with the odds and ends of Garibaldi's army wandering through the Vosges. On January 28, 1871, Paris fell; soon thereafter Garibaldi went home and Bartholdi resigned. In a black mood, the artist then determined to cross the Atlantic.

Bartholdi did not intend to leave his native land permanently. France, he had faith, would recover and rise to greater heights than ever. Other reasons led him to America.

No doubt he was curious to see the New World. Probably he also hoped to pick up some commissions that would cover his costs. But most of all he wanted to explore a project that had been turning over in his mind for some years.

In Paris Bartholdi had come to know Professor Edouard René Lefebvre de Laboulaye, whose bust he had completed in 1866. The professor was a distinguished legal scholar but also had strong political interests and was the center of a circle of liberal intellectuals into which the sculptor occasionally drifted. The talk was often of America, about which Laboulaye had written numerous books. Over and over, Bartholdi heard the same theme repeated: France and the United States were bound in friendship and had been for almost a century since they were allies during the American Revolution. Then too, when the conversation touched on the recent Civil War, it reached the conclusion that Americans had made and would continue to make tremendous sacrifices for the advancement of freedom. And again, whenever the discussion turned to local issues — the empire, Napoleon III, the need for a constitution — Laboulaye usually turned to the United States as a model.

Now in 1871, with France reeling from external defeat and bleeding internally from the suppression of the revolutionary Paris Commune, Bartholdi pursued a suggestion Laboulaye had once made — that a monument to commemorate American independence would testify to the friendship of a century. In the sculptor's imagination the torch moved from the lighthouse at Suez to a harbor in the United States; and the light that streamed forth was not that of western civilization to the East, but of liberty nurtured in the New World streaming back to show the way to the Old.

Everywhere Bartholdi went in the United States he talked about his project. Letters of introduction gave him access to influential men. In Long Branch, New

In his search for a physical representation of American liberty, Bartholdi studied the silver dollars that were in circulation at the time of his 1871 visit. Curiously enough, his final design bore less resemblance to the portly Liberty of those early coins (above, left and center) than to the prognathous profile of the 1879 Liberty (above right).

Jersey, he and President Ulysses S. Grant smoked their cigars in the little garden of the summer cottage, where the chief executive entertained his guest like a simple bourgeois. In Nahant, Massachusetts, the sculptor made several visits to Henry Wadsworth Longfellow and received amiable encouragement. In Washington, D. C., on the Fourth of July, Senator Charles Sumner took time to show the visitor about. The Parisian found the poor architecture and the negligible sculpture as depressing as the still unfinished Washington Monument on which nothing had been done for fifteen years.

But Bartholdi had not crossed the ocean to look at statues. Nor did he wish merely to sell his idea. Above all he sought to understand the people and the country, to gain insight into the American national character so that he could fill out his own grand idea. He did not find it easy to sort and appraise his impressions. He hastened to Chicago, San Francisco, Sacramento, Salt Lake, Denver, Saint Louis, and Pittsburgh. He saw plains, mountains, forests, bridges, viaducts, tunnels, sleeping cars, oil wells, and chimneys. Everything was big, even the peas; everything was on tracks, like the railroad; everything had a materialistic tone. All that was hard on the individual who did not wish simply to be carried along, who resented poor food eaten off counters in factory-like hotels without charm or taste. But on the other hand, the immense nation, in many ways savage and colossal, sustained an impartial government supported with admirable patriotism; and its people were animated by a strong sense of duty and a concern for education. Bartholdi was not philosopher enough to add up the results of his observations. But the memories returned to him frequently as he worked on his monumental project in the years to come.

The sculptor brought back to Paris, in the fall of 1871, a clear image of *Liberty Enlightening the World*, the monument he wished to raise on Bedloe's Island. But experience had by now taught him what a long way there was between the vision in the mind and the statue on its pedestal. There remained the tasks of raising the necessary funds, and of working out the design and the practical procedures for erecting the monument. The two aspects of the project had to proceed concurrently. Without money, the idea would never become a reality; and without the design to convince potential donors, no one would give a *sou*.

These were not the best of times for big undertakings in France. The new republic struggled uneasily to survive through the 1870's; to observers it seemed calamitously weak, its future precarious. The probability that it would remain a republic was slim, for the holders of power were monarchists in principle, held back from restoring a king only by the inglorious bickering of the three rival claimants for the throne that did not yet exist. Nevertheless tremendous energies were rising to the surface that soon touched off a renaissance in literature and in painting, gave expression to the concepts of vigorous thinkers, created an impressive industrial system, carried the French flag and interests to the far corners of Asia and Africa, and made Paris a world capital. The upsurge of energy provided the resources of both finance and technology to aid Bartholdi's project.

The intellectuals and politicians around Laboulaye who had originally planted the idea in Bartholdi's imagination remained the backbone of the organiza-

His quest for a corporeal means of expressing the abstract concept of liberty was to lead Bartholdi back to two obvious models time and time again. Those models were eventually fused into a single image of Liberty Enlightening the World — *one that combined the stern countenance of the sculptor's mother (seen in the 1855 portrait below at left) with the earthy voluptuousness of* Liberty Leading the People *(below), the central figure in Delacroix's enormous study of the civil uprising that gripped the French capital in late July of 1830.*

tion that assembled the resources to carry it out. Liberty was important to them, and the United States was the model of the constitutional regime they hoped France would develop — free yet operating within the restraints of law. In the 1870's both aspects needed defense, for conservatives attacked the excess of freedom that followed the downfall of the empire and radicals attacked the excess of law that followed the downfall of the Commune. America proved that the middle way was feasible. Laboulaye and his friends who upheld that position were not at the center of power, but they were influential and commanded the means of making their views known.

In 1875 the sponsors moved from talk to action. Bartholdi's cousin Philippe had become minister to the United States; and the Centennial Exhibition in Philadelphia — a year away — seemed an appropriate occasion for the presentation. John W. Forney, newspaper publisher and Republican politician, was in Paris publicizing the coming event. It was time to do something about the great idea. In August, Bartholdi finished a plaster model of the statue and Laboulaye formed the Franco-American Union. At a large dinner at the Hôtel du Louvre on November 6, the liberal politician launched the financial campaign in a speech that hailed the monument as a symbol of reciprocation: America held forth to Europe the liberty the New World had received from the Old.

Prominent friends of long standing were drawn to the cause instinctively. For the descendants of Lafayette, the transatlantic connection was a family tradition. Men with business ties to the United States or with projects that required the support of American opinion also participated in the Franco-American Union, among them the promoters of a canal across the Isthmus of Panama. They gave a distinguished tone to the membership list. But they did not expect to give the whole cost of the statue.

The initial appeal was rather aimed at the French municipalities, which were the usual sources of support for civic monuments. The dinner made the need known; private persuasion followed. Paris, Le Havre, and a few other cities, the Freemasons, and some business firms responded to the tune of some 200,000 francs, a respectable amount. But a grand fete at the Opera at which Charles Gounod conducted his cantata *La Liberté éclairant le monde,* on April 25, 1876, was poorly attended and brought in only 8,000 francs. The total from the gifts that thus dribbled in was far from the amount that Bartholdi's estimate now indicated was necessary. However attractive the notion of Franco-American friendship as a sentiment, the crusty provincial bourgeois were not overly generous with funds for a monument to grace a far-off harbor. They were after all slow to open their purses even to grace the local square. Evidently the monument would be far from ready by the time the Centennial Exhibition opened in Philadelphia — indeed, there had been little progress by the time it closed later that year.

Every sculptor was accustomed to such delays, and Bartholdi was not discouraged. The essential was to have enough cash on hand to keep up the momentum. Time would provide more when needed — somehow.

In 1879 the campaign for funds was resumed, directed this time at a wider pool of potential donors. The big scheme was a lottery. Prominent firms con-

tributed 538 valuable prizes to go to the holders of the lucky numbers, and 300,000 tickets went on sale in an appeal to the cupidity as well as the generosity of the middle classes. Other little schemes and a few large contributions brought in the remaining sums. On July 7, 1881, a notification dinner informed the Americans that the money to pay the costs of construction, the equivalent of some $400,000, was in hand. It had been a long time since the idea had first sprouted, a full decade since Bartholdi's exploratory visit to the United States, six years since the opening campaign. But the end was in sight, and meanwhile the sculptor had been at work, painfully bringing the monument into existence.

The creative task proved more difficult than the financial one. Bartholdi took for granted that it would be, but the actuality was more complex than he expected. It involved first a problem of imagination, then one of engineering. For instance, what did an abstract idea look like? "Liberty" or "virtue" or "knowledge" or "courage" could not directly take shape in stone or metal; by their very nature, concepts had no material shape or texture. To make them visible, the artist had to personify them, reduce them to a form recognizable by the beholder. Some associations were familiar: courage — dying soldier; knowledge — sage elder; virtue — innocent maiden. But liberty? What was the appearance of liberty?

Moreover, Bartholdi's theme was *American* liberty; the image he chose had to reflect the spirit of the New World and of its people. That was why he had considered his visit in 1871 important.

No existing conventional figure was appropriate.

Back in 1855, when he had begun work on the Bruat monument, Bartholdi had conceived of America as a young man — proud, almost savage — his arms resting on a machine, a horn of plenty at his side, and the shattered idols of the past at his feet. The emphasis was upon power and material strength; and ample evidence of that vigor had passed before the sculptor's eyes as he toured the continent. But those were not the qualities he now wished to stress.

Nor did familiar European images of liberty satisfy him. He knew Delacroix's famous painting of 1830 in which liberty was a flaming young woman, her clothes half torn away, leaping to the barricade over the bodies of fallen comrades. That was not it either; too violent, it conformed neither to the country he had seen nor to his own aspiration for constitutional freedom.

The picture of Columbia that commonly came to the minds of many Americans was closer, but not quite adequate. Derived from the lines of Joel Barlow's epic and imprinted on the face of coins, liberty thus portrayed was a Roman goddess — placid, remote from man, offering no hint of passion or involvement.

The statue that evolved from Bartholdi's imagination bore some resemblance to Columbia, although the antique robe and the upheld torch had also been in the Suez plan. The broken chains had antecedents in the Bruat monument. The law book, dated July 4, 1776, was new. But in the end, for a woman on whom to model the figure of liberty, Auguste turned to his mother — tall, powerful, a sheltering presence ever offering a refuge to those who needed comfort. The sculptor's skilled fingers, passing over the plaster, iden-tified those qualities with American liberty.

First the idea, then the shape small enough so the eye could take it in. Then an immense task of painstaking detail. The statue Bartholdi actually fashioned in a first plaster model was a little over four feet high. The one that would finally rise in New York harbor was to be 151 feet high, the face alone 10 feet wide. It remained to translate the statue into the monument.

The engineering problem itself was formidable. The great structure would have to bear its own weight and resist the force of any wind or tide that might sweep across the bay. It would also have to contain a mode of access to the flaming torch and rest firmly on a base that would keep it upright through the passing decades. For the calculations and structural advice Bartholdi called upon the engineer Alexandre Gustave Eiffel, who had not yet gained fame for the tower he would later erect on the Seine. Eiffel suggested an interior framework of iron, a frame upon which the exterior metal would be fastened. The surface of the statue would consist of hammered sheets — the first plans called for bronze; when that proved too heavy, pure copper, 3/32 of an inch thick, was substituted. Each sheet would be independently fastened by iron straps to beams that transferred its weight to the central framework.

In a cavernous workshop the sculptor supervised construction. Liberty did not rise from the toes upward, a fact that occasionally disconcerted skeptical or uninformed visitors who saw only detached segments in various stages of completion, here the head, there the arm, the torso in scattered portions. Bartholdi's preference determined the sequence of execution, as did the desire to have some finished elements to display to potential donors.

The technique was complicated. The original model was enlarged first to one-sixteenth and then to one-fourth the ultimate dimensions, each still not too large to be viewed as a whole, yet big enough to permit the perfection of detail. Then came the transfer. From some 300 main points on the second enlarged model, fine wires led to 1,200 points on four plaster sections that together would form the final monument. Around the precise copy thus created, workmen fitted boards which formed latticed molds, against which other craftsmen hammered the copper into shape with mallets. The laborious process yielded hundreds of separate sheets, which were then hung upon the iron framework Eiffel had contrived. By the beginning of 1883, hundreds of Parisians came on Sundays to visit the yards of Gaget, Gauthier & Company, to watch the statue take form and to cheer the impromptu orators who took advantage of the chance audiences to eulogize the happy land across the ocean. Early in 1884, Liberty finally raised her head high over the roofs of Paris, ready for her move to a site in the New World. In a great presentation ceremony on July 4, 1884, France formally handed over the completed statue to the United States.

By then the French government was ready to put all its resources behind the delivery. The country had regained its strength and the middle classes and the peasants at least were prosperous. But the republic was still not secure, for reaction remained a threat. Perhaps that was why the new regime was willing to support a gesture that would gain international good will and thus emphasize the importance of liberty.

In December, the work of getting Liberty over the ocean began. The statue was dismantled and her pieces packed in forty-nine mammoth wooden cases, while the iron work fitted into thirty-six others. Months of effort went into taking the structure apart, labeling each segment, and anchoring it carefully. Then special trucks hauled the 500,000 pounds of wood and metal to the Gare Saint-Lazare, from which a train of seventy cars carried it to Rouen. In the middle of May 1885 Liberty was ready to be taken by the warship *Isère* to America.

As she waited, she was evidence of the power of an idea that had moved Bartholdi and Laboulaye and all those who had participated in the creation of the monument. The liberty to which the United States had made an important contribution was a need of the modern world, in 1885 as for two centuries before and, many believed, for years to come.

Pierre Auguste Renoir produced this lambent study of the Pont Neuf in 1872, at a time when Paris was in a state of political and artistic ferment unequaled since the High Renaissance. Stunned and outraged by the twin humiliations of Metz and Sedan, the citizens of Paris had risen against Louis Napoleon's feeble regime, seized the capital, and established the Commune of 1871. Famine and factiousness toppled that government in turn, and by 1872 monarchists, Socialists, and Radical Republicans were all jockeying for power. The frenetic atmosphere of the period was recorded by a small group of dissident artists — among them Monet, Pissarro, Cezanne, Degas, and Manet — whom one scornful wag had labeled "impressionists." Banned from official exhibitions and reviled by the established critics, these intrepid artists took to showing their paintings in private. Such creative fervor, coupled with vigorous rejection of conventional artistic credos, must have infected Bartholdi when he returned to France in 1871, for he resumed his drive to raise funds for the statue with renewed vigor. The money raised, Bartholdi turned to the prodigious task of constructing the colossal figure itself.

II

THE MEANING OF LIBERTY

The statue was a monument — both a metal artifact and a symbol. It existed in the packing cases on board the *Isère* and also in the mind of the artist who gave it form. The copper plates, reassembled, would rise in New York harbor. The symbol was and remained a vision of Europeans.

So too, America was both an actual place and also a symbol. It existed as a fact of geography. It existed also in the imaginations of Europeans, many of whom like Laboulaye never actually set eyes on it, but for whom it served a need. For centuries before 1885 and for generations after that year, America represented the idea of liberty and exemplified its meaning.

With the waning of the Middle Ages, restless Europeans had turned their gaze outward, and had begun to probe the spaces to the east and to the west of their own continent. At first the movement involved a small minority of men unwilling to accept as fixed the society and the culture into which they had been born. Often they did not know what they sought, except that it was something different from what they had. They contrived legends of the Holy Grail; they wandered in pilgrimages; and for a time they embarked on the great emotional movements that were known as the Crusades. Or, like Marco Polo, they used trade as an excuse for escape to a far place. An uneasy compulsion urged them on, although to what destination was not clear.

At some point during the Renaissance a myth developed and supplied the seekers with a new goal. Somewhere, hidden and unknown, was an earthly paradise, a perfect land that would fully satisfy its discoverer. In its perfection it differed from every land already known. From visionary dreamers the belief

Bartholdi's first model of Liberty's head

spread to practical people. Soldiers, mariners, merchants, and statesmen began to believe that there was a place where all the problems of the society about them dissolved in golden satisfactions.

Columbus had set forth on his momentous journey of 1492 in quest of that earthly paradise. Persuaded that the pear-shaped territory actually existed somewhere south of China, he hit upon the hitherto unknown continents that obstructed his course across the ocean. The dawning awareness of the meaning of his discovery gave an altogether new turn to the speculations of Europeans. That landfall, it became clear, had been neither in China nor in the Indies nor in any familiar portion of the globe. It had come in an altogether new and therefore tremendously exciting world, one that offered immense scope for the play of men's imaginations.

In the series of journeys and migrations that followed, Europeans tried to exploit the real and fancied riches of America. But the discovery also set off adventurous intellectual explorations. What was new about the New World was the fact that it was not the Old World. In other words, it could satisfy the need for a magic mirror of contrasts, into which Europeans could look to see what was wrong with the life they actually led.

These speculations long revolved about the question of divine intentions with regard to America. In an age of faith, there were disputes about creeds and rituals but not about the fundamental proposition that every occurrence was an expression of God's will. Europeans therefore had to ask themselves why the Lord had so long withheld this vast territory from their knowledge.

It could not be by accident; an omnipotent Creator permitted no casual oversights in his schemes. The concealment of America, and then its discovery, had some deliberate, purposeful intention. The exhilarating conclusion followed logically: God had hidden this fortunate corner of the earth to provide the setting for a totally new chapter in human history. Here the future would reveal its mysterious shape.

In the eighteenth century the meaning Europeans ascribed to the term America narrowed dramatically. The word, even when used by Spaniards and Frenchmen, certainly when used by Englishmen, ceased to refer to Mexico or Peru, to Jamaica or Canada. Those places had lost much of their newness and in many ways had become offshoots of Europe. Increasingly in common usage, the name America was applied to the colonies between Florida and Maine in which a novel society had developed. There Europeans could make out the outlines of the future, test their predictions of what was to come, and thus express their dissatisfaction with the present.

Information about America came from settlers and from promoters who wished to stimulate settlement. In the 1680's a flood of tracts in English, French, Dutch, and German appeared in Europe. Put forth by agents of William Penn, they promised people willing to cross the Atlantic a haven where the poor could live in peace and plenty, make their own laws, pay only the taxes to which they themselves consented, and worship as they wished. Cheap or free land drew thousands across, and their letters back home to Europe often enough confirmed what the pamphlets said to make credible the picture of a New World paradise.

33

Bartholdi's Liberty was virtually complete by 1884, the year that Auguste Rodin began work on his own tribute to liberty, a powerful and haunting statue group known as The Burghers of Calais. *In the hands of France's pre-eminent sculptor, Bartholdi's abstract theme was transmuted and humanized in a manner so forthright and compelling that it both disturbed and dismayed the men who commissioned it. Those latter-day burghers of Calais had wanted a heroic memorial to their famed forebears, the six selfless citizens who surrendered to Edward III of England in 1347 to save their besieged city from imminent devastation. What Rodin delivered, after months of testy negotiation, was a breathtakingly unconventional grouping that underscored the medieval burghers' intense personal agony.*

The favorable view of the land colored the Europeans' conception of its aboriginal inhabitants. In Alexander Pope's *Essay on Man* (1733), the Indian was the Noble Savage whose untutored mind saw God in clouds or heard him in the wind. Untaught by science, he received his hope of heaven from simple Nature.

The comments of travelers were more dispassionate. Peter Kalm, a Swedish naturalist who visited the colonies in the middle of the eighteenth century, observed the strange beasts and plants, noticed the habits and manners of the population, and supplied the material for an extended debate in Europe. His information led many to wonder whether America did or did not provide a favorable environment for human development.

Influential writers argued that colonization was a mistake. "Men should stay where they are," in harmony with their natural surroundings, wrote Montesquieu. The French naturalist Buffon, the Dutchman Cornelius DePauw, and the Abbé Reynal, whose influential history of European overseas settlement went into thirty-seven editions between 1770 and 1820, all supported the case against migration. The native Indian tribes had produced an inferior civilization; the French, Spaniards, and Portuguese had been corrupted by contact with America; and after two centuries of settlement, the Western Hemisphere had produced no great universities and not a man of genius in any art or science.

Along came Benjamin Franklin, living evidence of what the defenders of America had long been arguing. That formidable polemicist Voltaire, for instance, had made the New World the idealized image of what he wished France to be — a country of peace and equality,

not dominated by priests, and guaranteeing religious freedom to all. "That golden age of which men talk so much," he told his readers, "probably never existed anywhere except in Pennsylvania." Franklin was the proof — a printer's boy who needed no university to become a distinguished scientist and man of letters. He exemplified in Paris the rural virtues, the basis of true liberty, which even the queen, Marie Antoinette, understood when she played at being a milkmaid. The description Franklin gave of his country showed that in America the ideas of the Enlightenment had been put into practice: the faith in reason — every American farmer read not only a newspaper but a work of philosophy or politics every day; progress — the colonies, only yesterday a wilderness, were on the way to being a great nation; humanitarianism — the common man, trusted with freedom, made responsible use of it.

The most influential intellectuals of Europe were persuaded; this after all was what they wished to believe. Their own ideas were not only true but practical. James Burgh and Richard Price in England joined the French in celebrating the achievement of the Americans as a means of inducing the Old World to adopt the reforms they advocated. Let but the old regime abolish censorship, allow freedom of religion, remove restrictions on trade, ease the burden of taxes — and the same beneficent results would follow in Europe as in the colonies.

Few of the writers who appealed to the transatlantic model had actually laid eyes on the New World, but the lack of firsthand information did not slow the flow of words. It was easier to discuss America than France or Britain. The royal censors and judges would not allow Voltaire or Burgh directly to attack the established church or the monarchy or the legal system, but they rarely interfered with volumes about a remote continent. The encyclopedist Diderot was surprised at the open publication of one such work which, he believed, would instruct people in their inalienable rights and inspire in them a love of liberty. Because the book was about the colonies, the censors did not conceive that it was addressed to all men. "They allow us to read things like this, and they are amazed to find us ten years later different men. Do they not realize how easily noble souls must drink of these principles and become intoxicated by them?"

In 1776 praise for America as a means toward the end of criticizing Europe became praise for its own sake. The Revolution and the principles upon which it rested demonstrated the validity of the arguments of a century past. No doubt for Louis XVI and his ministers, as for George III and his, the whole episode was part of a continuing struggle for empire. But the intellectuals and their followers viewed the issue differently. The Declaration of Independence, out of respect for the opinion of mankind, had explained the issue and was believed. Here man cast off the chains of tyranny and embraced liberty. Unrestrained by the bonds of the feudal past, he sought to shape his own destiny, form his own society, and create a government to uphold his natural rights. The Revolution was the work not of a mob but of people concerned with a higher law than that of kings, the law of nature. The drama that culminated in the framing of the Constitution was thus an illustration of the practicality of the political theories of Locke and Rousseau, a grand event

in the history of mankind. The lesson had implications everywhere. The Marquis de Condorcet noted that enthusiasm about the liberty of a foreign people gave his countrymen an opportunity to avow publicly sentiments that caution usually prevented them from expressing. He concluded that they would not wait long to recover their own freedom.

Actual contacts during the War for Independence made Europeans aware that the New World bred not only a different political system but also a different kind of man. The adventurers and idealists, like Lafayette, who volunteered to fight with the colonists were sometimes disappointed in the lack of recognition and the skimpy rewards they received, but nevertheless they were aware that they were involved in a challenging new experience. They encountered a strange kind of soldier not necessarily better than, but unlike, the mercenaries or conscripts of Pomerania or Gascony. Baron von Steuben wrote back to a friend in Europe: "You say to your soldier, 'Do this,' and he does it; but I am obliged to say, 'This is the reason why you ought to do that'; and then he does it." Americans thought for themselves and acted not by obedience to authority but out of conviction. Therefore they were willing to endure danger and boredom, to live on little, and to go without pleasure for the sake of a cause. The thousands of French troops who fought as allies, the thousands of Hessians who fought as enemies, encountered in the lanes of Newport and Yorktown, in the countryside of Pennsylvania and Virginia, a way of life, that was attractive to them because it was free of habit, tradition, and imposed restraints.

The memories they brought back with them made

Bartholdi's unsung collaborator — the man who designed the ingenious load-bearing framework of the statue. — was Gustave Eiffel (right), designer of the "beloved monstrosity" that bears his name. Eiffel himself referred to the tower (seen under construction at far right) as "the tallest flagpole in the world"; many critics took an even dimmer view of the soaring spire.

credible the idyllic description of an influential book published in 1782, the *Letters from an American Farmer*, by J. Hector St. John Crèvecoeur. Crèvecoeur was a Frenchman who lived in Canada and New York and had returned to his native land in 1780. He raised questions and gave answers to which his contemporaries were attentive.

Who was this new man, the American? He was the product of a mixture of English, Scottish, Irish, French, Dutch, German, and Swedish elements. "From this promiscuous breed, that race, now called Americans, have arisen." By what power was this surprising metamorphosis performed? "By that of the laws and that of the people's industry." *He* is an American who, leaving behind him all his ancient prejudices and manners, receives new ones from the new mode of life he has embraced, the new government he obeys, and the new rank he holds. Here individuals of all nations are melted into a new race of men, whose labors and posterity will one day cause great changes in the world. Crèvecoeur's prediction reverberated most audibly through the remainder of the eighteenth century; but its echoes brought hope to millions of Europeans for many decades more.

The makers of the French Revolution after 1789 were very much conscious of American experience. Thomas Paine, among others, hastened back to the Old World to participate in that revolution as he had in the other. But 1789 was not 1776, and France was not the United States; nor did revolution in the Old World proceed as it had in the New. The removal of Louis XVI led to Napoleon's empire and then to the restoration of the Bourbons. This puzzling outcome

raised the question of whether the experience of America really was applicable to Europe. Furthermore, the first republic did not come to the aid of the second in the conflicts with the monarchs of the old regime during the 1790's; nor, however lavish its sympathies with revolution, would the United States offer aid to the uprisings that disturbed the Continent in the nineteenth century.

Some thinkers concluded that the New World was indeed a fortunate exception. "America, you have it better . . ." began a well-known poem by Goethe. The United States was the only case in history, concluded Madame de Staël, in which an enlightened people was able to enjoy both liberty and equality. In the darker moments of the cause of European liberalism, when the prospects of imitation seemed slight, even then the transatlantic republic could serve, as Diderot had earlier suggested, as "an asylum for all the people of Europe from fanaticism and tyranny." In the brighter moments, hope survived that America would yet be the model, either in the violent uprisings that swept across the Continent in 1830 and 1848 or in the gradual evolution toward constitutional regimes everywhere.

From 1815 to 1914, from Waterloo to Sarajevo, from the Congress of Vienna to the invasion of Belgium when the lights went out over Europe, an uneasy balance between conservatives and liberals prevailed. It was to add weight to the side of liberty that Laboulaye conceived of and Bartholdi executed the monument.

The monarchs of the Continent, fearful of a repetition of the suffering of the quarter-century of violence before 1815, were determined to suppress the wicked tendencies that threatened to plunge society into re-

Constructed in 1889 to commemorate
the one-hundredth anniversary of the
French Revolution, the Eiffel Tower
touched off a protracted and heated
debate among visitors to the Centennial
Exposition. Gustave Eiffel's edifice was
clearly an engineering triumph. But was
the world's tallest structure also an
eyesore? The Parisian press insisted that
it was — but Parisian artists soon proved
those critics wrong. Pierre Bonnard,
for example, made the graceful sweep
of the tower the focal point of his 1912
cityscape (right), and Marc Chagall set
the structure off with klieg lights in
his characteristically dreamlike view of
nighttime Paris (above). Pierre Delaunay's
infatuation with Eiffel's creation was
so complete that he seldom painted
anything else, preferring to fix his full
attention on the iron tracery of the
tower, which his mind's eye warped into
dozens of new shapes (above right).
Perhaps the loveliest view of the
tower is Georges Seurat's 1890 study
of the slender shaft (opposite) outlined
against a shimmering sky.

newed disorder. They knew that they could not crush the American experiment, but they believed that they could limit and contain the contagion. The Holy Alliance, created by Prince Metternich of Austria and Tsar Alexander I of Russia, aimed to staunch the influence of radical ideas and revolutionary movements in the European states and their possessions, by strengthening established institutions, by repressing dissent, and by isolating their own countries from the United States.

Their system endured through the nineteenth century, although under forms that changed with the passage of time. For almost two decades after 1850, Napoleon III was the central figure in the struggle to restrain liberal influence. His secret police kept him informed of possible conspiracies in America as well as in Europe; and the hope of outflanking the threat of republicanism was one element in his espousal of the cause of the Confederacy during the Civil War as well as of his sponsorship of an ill-fated Mexican empire for his Habsburg puppet Maximilian.

Napoleon's downfall in 1870 shifted the responsibility to other hands — those of the Russian tsars, the German kaisers, and the Austrian emperor. The emergence of a liberal, national Italian state worried the Catholic Church; by the 1890's, influential figures in Rome believed that an American heresy was a serious danger, and the papal bull *Testem Benevolentiae* aimed to crush the seed before it produced too many troublesome weeds.

The Baron von Hübner, an Austrian diplomat who traveled through the United States in 1871, the same year as Bartholdi, stated the conservative case simply.

America is the "classic soil of liberty and equality, and
it has become so from the fact that it was peopled by
men whom Europe expelled." It is therefore "the born
antagonist of Europe," hostile to the "fundamental
principles of society." Those who value those principles
dread the success of the New World experiment and
"as far as they can they try to stop the spread" of ideas
emanating from it.

But Hübner perceived that the friends of the United
States were in the great majority. They found across
the ocean the prototype of a higher civilization and
wished to transform themselves after the American example. They saw in the Republic a society without
kings or nobility, without censors or an established
church, without guilds, licenses, great armies, and oppressive taxes — that is, without all the features they
called feudal, which blocked the development of their
own countries. And decade after decade the success of
the New World experiment heartened reformers and
revolutionaries in Europe.

The movements for national reconstruction that
named themselves Young Italy or Young Ireland longed
for the vigor and the freedom from past error that
seemed characteristic of America. Their leaders were
like Mazzini, constitutionalists firm in the belief that
a written frame of government similar to if not identical with that of the United States would provide a
foundation of freedom everywhere, sweeping away the
ancient rubbish of history yet holding back the destructive forces that had ruined the French Revolution.
Laboulaye and his circle belonged in this company and
they had counterparts among the intellectuals and
business people of Germany, Poland, Hungary, and

Scandinavia — indeed, of all the lands without free institutions. There were even faint echoes in the tsar's
domains, and Russian exiles like Aleksandr Herzen
responded eagerly to the lure of the American model.
All these people saw across the Atlantic the political
liberty for which they themselves desperately longed.

The revolutions of 1848, which incorporated many
of these longings, were a turning point. On the face
of it, they were failures. In France, the overthrow of
Louis Philippe led in the end only to the tawdry reach
for glory of Napoleon III's empire. The idealists who
dreamed of a German parliament lived to see unifica-
tion achieved through Prussian blood and iron. Hungarian nationalism flowered not into Lajos Kossuth's
liberal state but into a partnership with Austria at the
expense of the Slavic provinces. Italy became a kingdom, not a republic, and Ireland remained under
British rule while a majority of its population fled
overseas.

These circumstances gave point to warnings about
the dangers of following American precedent. De
Tocqueville had already sounded a pessimistic note.
Democracy in the United States emphasized equality
rather than freedom and threatened to substitute the
tyranny of mass conformity for the rule of an established order. Hübner pointed to the fundamental differences between the Old World and the New. The
one lacked space, which the other possessed in abundance. The one could only gradually rebuild, the other
started afresh. "To become American would be to pre-
suppose the entire destruction of Europe."

European change after 1850 was slow and controlled.
National states altered the map of the Continent and

Visitors to Bartholdi's Parisian warehouse-workshop
were astonished by the chaotic and seemingly haphazard
manner in which the statue was being constructed.
Work proceeded piecemeal — a fact that stunned casual
onlookers, who expected the mammoth statue to rise
as a recognizable whole. The complex task of scaling
up Bartholdi's first model involved a three-step
conversion, the final stages of which can be seen in
these contemporary photographs. By the winter of
1882, the sculptor's assistants had enlarged the original
to one-sixteenth, then one-fourth its final size. They
then began the tedious task of erecting a full-scale
model of lath and lumber (right) that dwarfed its
creators. The panoramic view below reveals both the
penultimate and the final models of Liberty's left hand
— as well as a quarter-size head.

parliamentary regimes appeared everywhere west of Russia, and even there, after the turn of the century. There was some amelioration of the condition of the most oppressed groups. But the essential fabric of society remained intact. The monarchy, the aristocracy, the established churches and professions retained their privileges and made only slight concessions to the spirit of the times. The Old World in 1914 was far from Americanized.

The adverse drift of European events did not alter the favorable views of America. Actually, for intellectuals like Laboulaye the golden land across the Atlantic glistened all the more brightly by contrast with the shadows that fell across his hopes for his own country. He and people like him expressed their faith in books. Others, in the millions, expressed it in migration; decade after decade until 1914, men, women, and children from every corner of Europe chose freedom and America.

The great Civil War that tore the Union apart between 1861 and 1865 tested the weight of those sentiments. The European conservatives watched with glee what they hoped would be the proof of the failure of republican government. Interest and ideology combined to attach their sympathy to the Confederacy. But the liberals and their cohorts understood that the cause of the Union was the last, best hope of common men everywhere, not only insofar as it involved the abolition of slavery but also insofar as it tested the workability of democratic institutions. Laboulaye, for one, threw every energy into defense of the United States; and across the Channel that formidable liberal John Bright mobilized English opinion on the same side.

43

Most impressive were the expressions of support from laboring men, including those thrown out of work by the closing of the cotton mills, who understood where their larger interest lay.

Abraham Lincoln was a comic character in the newspapers and magazines the upper-class Europeans read — most savagely depicted as an apelike barbarian; more kindly, as an uncouth rustic. To the mass of men, in Europe as in America, he presented an entirely different aspect. He was one of them, though he held power; he had known life through the rude work of his own hands; and the dark lineaments of his sad face showed that he like they had tasted the tragedies of the human condition. But the mass of men did not write clever articles or draw amusing pictures and remained unheard.

Only with the news of the assassination did the voices usually quiet make themselves heard. All the governments, of course, delivered the expected notes of condolence. Less expected was the sense of popular emotional shock throughout Europe. John Bigelow, United States minister in Paris, wrote that he had until then no idea of the depth of public feeling about the martyred president. It was not the usual business of diplomats to know what the baker or cobbler felt; but on this occasion the communication got through. The loss of Lincoln was a loss to all men, because it was a loss to the liberty that America represented.

In this context, Bartholdi's extraordinary enterprise made sense. It rested upon the hopes Europeans had long attached and would continue to attach to the New World. Whatever occurred in the Old World, liberty was secure in the New; and in time it would enlighten the whole world. Its significance was universal; the

By the spring of 1883, Bartholdi was ready to begin assembling the preformed components of his huge statue on the scaffolding that had been erected outside his Paris workshop. Under Liberty's disembodied gaze (above), workmen began hoisting the copper plates into place — and within a few months the first half of their task had been completed (opposite).

replicas of the monument that appeared, not only in Paris but far off in Hanoi, were symbols of a promise valid for everyone. The cause of America, Thomas Paine had said, was the cause of all mankind. A century later, that faith still endured.

Radicals, who went beyond the liberals in their demand for social and economic as well as political change, conceded that the United States did not suffer from the same faults as Europe. The anarchist Bakunin who visited the New World was amazed by the extent to which the people of America seemed to have escaped the troubles that beset the people of the Old World. And Karl Marx from time to time gave a good deal of thought to the question of whether the Republic was an exception to the general rules of capitalist development. On the whole, he tended to think, it was not; but still he recognized its differences from the lands where the old regimes remained intact, and he conceded the possibility that it might evolve toward socialism by democratic means.

Hopes that the United States would exercise a beneficent effect upon the future of Europe reached their climax during and just after World War I. Then, when all countries were exhausted by the struggle, when society everywhere was in disarray, when the problem of winding up the bloody conflict for the moment turned men's attention from the still greater problem of reconstruction that lay ahead, then appeared the young nation still untouched by tragedy, still vigorous in the abundance of its resources and manpower. Toward it all thoughts drew in the longing for peace and rebuilding.

The appearance of the first doughboys in France rejoiced the hearts of the Allies, as evidence of the

While half of Bartholdi's assistants scaled the scaffold to assemble Liberty's torso (above), a second crew bolted the arm and torch together in the warehouse yard. As summer became fall, the workmen's task drew to a close: the statue's head was lifted into place (opposite), and final preparations were made to raise the arm and torch into their proper position.

strength that would bring victory. The arrival of President Woodrow Wilson almost two years later gladdened the hearts of victors and vanquished alike. Into the devastation that was Europe his words cast the first rays of light: the war-weary everywhere recalled his phrases — the Fourteen Points of a just peace without victory, one that would conclude the war to end war and make the world safe for democracy. Here at last was the opportunity for fulfillment of the promise attached to Bartholdi's monument, Liberty from America Enlightening the World.

Frustration and disillusion followed; and a subtle alteration in opinion gradually wore away the favorable reputation of America in Europe.

Many factors contributed to the change. No doubt any peace would have disappointed some who attached high hopes to the outcome of the war. But the Treaty of Versailles was particularly vulnerable in the compromises that formed an ironic contrast to Wilson's eloquent words. The more extravagant the expectations, the more bitter was the taste of actuality.

Furthermore, by the 1920's the United States no longer seemed an exception to the rule that governed other countries. An industrialized urban society replaced the virtuous farm life of the past; the American flag had carried not liberty but imperialist control to foreign shores; racist views ran counter to traditional ideas of equality, degrading the Negro and excluding the immigrants; and fierce labor struggles showed that the Republic was not exempt from the class struggle.

In this light, the American isolationism of the 1920's appeared to be the diplomatic counterpart of the hedonism that prevailed within the country. Now the big

news out of the west was of bathtub gin and the hypocrisy of prohibition, of jazzy nightclubs and Hollywood scandals, of the antimonkey trial in Tennessee and lynchings in Alabama. When Bertolt Brecht wished to portray a society where moralizing was a cloak for materialistic self-interest, he set the *Rise and Fall of the Town Mahagonny* in the United States.

The critical message came from American as well as from European writers. The novelists of the lost generation, who sometimes made their homes in Paris and London, loudly proclaimed their disillusion; their very exile was evidence that home was no longer Eden but was poisoned by corruption. Twentieth-century literature going back to Jack London, Frank Norris, and Theodore Dreiser and extending on through Ernest Hemingway and F. Scott Fitzgerald told the same sordid story, confirmed by the journalistic reports of Lincoln Steffens, Upton Sinclair, and the muckrakers. Everything was rotten at the core — the cities, the towns, industry, the farms, politics, the universities. Europeans reading the books of these American authors absorbed mostly the shocking revelations and missed the note of yearning for a lost innocence and the affirmative hopes of redemption they often contained.

Then again, events in Europe also drew men's attention away from the liberty the New World offered. On the one hand, new models of the future appeared, many evolving out of a stream of socialist thought for which there was no American counterpart. England, France, and Scandinavia pioneered in schemes of social welfare legislation and developed powerful labor organizations; and Russia, Italy, and Germany harbored Communist, Fascist, and Nazi movements, which asserted a powerful claim on the loyalties of people who needed hope. On the other hand, the parliamentary regimes fashioned along liberal constitutional lines proved ineffective; Kerensky's government, the squabbling parties of postwar Italy, and the Weimar Republic inspired few Europeans with confidence. Men and women suffering from war and inflation now looked for solutions to the east rather than to the west. After all, gullible Americans too visited the Soviet Union and thought they saw the future at work or came back from Mussolini's country lavish with praise for trains that ran on time.

Between 1919 and 1939 the light that flashed from the Statue of Liberty's torch seemed to have lost its radiance. Its guardians, immersed in their own affairs, gave little thought to outsiders and allowed the flame to flicker untended. Europeans began to doubt that the New World had promise for them too.

Yet sparks continued to glow in remote places. From the stage of the Osvobozene Theater in Prague, Jan Werich and George Voskovec sang in 1939:

> If it hadn't been for Columbia
> The world's history would have been flat.
> I wish I had a submarine to go to New York
> And sing for the whole of Europe:
> Behold this great statue,
> Its head in the sky
> Its feet in the sea
> It's the Statue of Liberty!
> This is where the middle ages end:
> Europe's today was here yesterday.
> A country of freedom and work
> A country of civilization. . . .

That year the streets of Prague had already heard the invaders' boots, which soon would tramp through other cities as well. Soon men's hopes would again turn across the Atlantic and again find an answer. During the second and greater war and during the second and harder peace, the ships that carried men and aid out and that brought refugees in passed once more by Bartholdi's monument.

But the emotional tie between America and Europe did not recover the innocent strength of the nineteenth century. The New World was not so new, nor its promises as alluring as they had once been; and the scrawled "Yankee Go Home" on many a wall expressed the desire of a belligerent minority to follow a different light. Nor were Americans themselves sure of their purposes in the world. There was not an immediate reversion to the isolationism of the 1920's but neither was there the serene confidence of an earlier era that they marched in the vanguard of human progress toward enlightenment.

And when new invaders appeared in Prague, in tanks and not on foot, the United States knew that it could only deplore the event and offer asylum to a few of its victims.

III

THE LADY ARRIVES

During his first trip to America in 1871, Bartholdi met with nothing but cordial approval for his plan. He came equipped with letters from Laboulaye, whose writings were well-known in the United States, and his bearing and conversation were amiable. The sculptor talked about the monument, which expressed admiration for the country, and without intending to do so flattered his hosts. Longfellow and Sumner did not need to be told that the Republic extended the light of liberty to the rest of the world, but it was nice to hear it from an objective foreigner. Then too, Bartholdi made it clear that the statue would be a gift from the people of France. Approval was not even expensive. Bartholdi returned to Paris with the warm glow of all the assurances of cooperation he had received. And the Americans promptly proceeded to forget about the whole matter.

Accustomed to grandiose visions, Americans had learned that it was not always necessary to do anything about them. Sometimes, they worked out; in less than twenty years, 1850–70, a vast railroad network spanned the continent. Sometimes, the schemes simmered at the back of the stove for decade after decade; neither the Federal Capitol nor the Washington Monument, started years before, was yet finished. Sometimes, luck solved old problems, sometimes not. Only those could afford the luxury of unlimited dreams who knew how to distinguish them from reality. For a long time, nothing happened.

In 1875, when the Franco-American Committee in Paris launched its appeal for funds, a few Americans lent their names to the project, among them William M. Evarts, the New York lawyer and politician, and

The torch and hand on view in Philadelphia in 1876

Ambassador Elihu B. Washburne. It was a matter of making and listening to speeches, attending an occasional dinner, and giving moral support.

A year later, the pace quickened. Bartholdi then came to Philadelphia as a member of the French delegation to the Centennial Exhibition. The statue was far from ready, but at the Fourth of July parade in New York City, Bartholdi displayed a great transparency on which Liberty appeared as she finally would stand in the harbor; and on the same day he went out to Bedloe's Island to sketch the exact placement of the statue. Six weeks later a full-scale model of the arm and torch arrived in Philadelphia and drew the admiration of mobs of viewers. Thirteen feet high, it could support twelve men standing around the rim of the torch. Later it went on exhibition in New York. The project was becoming serious.

Now it attracted the attention of skeptical critics. Why just the arm? asked *The New York Times*, which sniffed at fraud. The proper place to begin was with the feet. Beware of the foreign slicker selling an implausible scheme. A chill developed in New York with the suggestion that Americans pay the cost of the pedestal. It was too expensive and what use did it serve anyway?

Long experience in dealing with French municipal councils had taught Bartholdi how to handle problems of this sort. He put the word about among his acquaintances in Philadelphia: perhaps that city would like to be the site of the monument. The news got back to New York. The *Times* hastened to explain: it had no doubt but that Liberty belonged in the port on the Hudson and anyway the statue would be useful as a

kind of lighthouse. Bartholdi was congenial. Yes, New York was the better site — only there was the problem of finding money for the pedestal.

A round of dinners followed in which everyone reassured everyone else and then, on January 2, 1877, at a meeting in the Century Club, a committee took shape under William M. Evarts and set to work. At the end of that month Bartholdi returned to Paris, quite satisfied that the American end of the project was well under control.

The committee, however, did not immediately turn its attention to the indelicate question of cash. Instead, it devoted its energies to implicating the federal government. As a result of its influence a Congressional resolution in January and a law in March authorized the president to accept the statue when finished, to place it on Governor's or Bedloe's Island, and to maintain it as a memorial commemorating French aid during the Revolution. That task accomplished, the distinguished members of the committee shifted their attention elsewhere.

More than three years had passed when the news arrived, in July 1881, of a dinner in Paris at which Bartholdi announced that the monument would be ready in 1883, in time for the centennial of the end of the War for Independence. It was time to get the pedestal up. The somnolent committee bestirred itself — to another dinner, this time at the Union League Club, on November 22, 1881. The appeal for funds went out. By then the plans prepared by the distinguished architect Richard M. Hunt were available and indicated that construction would take nine months and would cost well over the original estimate of

$125,000. The dinner was ample but the results were meager. Very little cash came in.

The truth was simple. The techniques for financing public projects were primitive. The sponsors meant well, but they were busy with other, more important affairs. The call for contributions launched into a vacuum fell flat; philanthropy still meant an action by an individual to support a cause that demonstrated his virtue, not participation in a common effort for which no single person felt responsible. In any case, another year and more went by and the statue was still not ready, which eased the pressure on the American committee.

But Bartholdi grew uneasy as his work approached completion in Paris. In 1883 he sent over three thousand autographs, hoping they could be sold to souvenir seekers; and a stream of letters nagged his friends into getting on with their work. The committee dutifully responded by reprinting its appeal and by asking communities throughout the nation to form subcommittees to gather gifts. The suggestion set the provinces to snickering. New York was rich enough to provide its own pedestal. Enough money came in to begin the work, not enough to finish it. A little railroad was built to move the stone about, and on July 20, 1884, the ferry *Bartholdi* made its first trip, shuttling supplies to Bedloe's Island. But the sum in hand was still far from sufficient to assure completion of the pedestal.

The World intervened. In 1883 that little newspaper changed hands. It had belonged to Jay Gould, the stock speculator and railroad and telegraph promoter, who had used it as a means of manipulating opinion.

Noted American jurist William M. Evarts (right) was embroiled in a campaign to break the Tweed Ring's stranglehold on New York City politics when he was called upon to launch a drive to raise funds for the statue's pedestal, but he accepted the added task without hesitation. Nearly a decade elapsed before those funds could be raised, however, and the pedestal was not completed until April 1886. By that time Evarts had been elected to the Senate from New York and Bartholdi and his monument had been immortalized on the sides of a special commemorative medal (opposite), struck to celebrate the statue's unveiling.

Its circulation was small; its reputation, rather shady. As its influence waned, it ceased to be useful to its owner and Gould tired of steadily losing money on it. On May 9, 1883, it passed into the hands of Joseph Pulitzer, quite a different character. On the surface at least.

Pulitzer came out of the Midwest. He had been in the United States some twenty years by then and had made good. But he still recalled the bitter years that had preceded success. A puny youth back in Hungary, he saw no future for himself in his native land; he was not even good enough for the ranks of the imperial army and had compiled quite a record of rejections by the recruiting officers of various countries on the Continent. But the American army was not so selective, for the Civil War consumed manpower at a voracious rate; and Pulitzer not only got to the New World with his passage paid but by making a smart deal collected an extra bounty as well. Military service had been difficult and the first years after demobilization were painful. But Pulitzer landed on his feet in Saint Louis. He turned his hand to this and that, made connections in the German-American community, dabbled in politics, and began to grow wealthy as a newspaper publisher. He married a girl of a good Washington, D.C. family, amassed a substantial stake, and in 1883 was ready to bid for national prominence. Purchase of the *World* that year was Pulitzer's first step toward doing so.

The new proprietor understood one thing: the paper had to become known and to make it known he would have to play upon the opinion of the public. Like Gould, he believed in the power of the informa-tion and values spread through society by word of mouth or the printed page, and he wished to grasp some of that power. But unlike Gould, Pulitzer also had to believe in the accuracy of the information and the worth of the values he disseminated. A *good cause* was therefore crucial in 1883 as it was later in Pulitzer's career. Once persuaded that he was right, he would in clear conscience go to any length of sensationalism in making the case, swaying people's minds, and persuading them to buy the *World*.

Liberty was a good cause. Nobody could doubt it. And the committee was a tempting target. Men of wealth often were, but never so much as when bumbling from dinner to dinner achieving nothing.

Blast! On May 14, 1883, a *World* editorial attacked the millionaires of New York who spent fortunes on their own luxuries but stood around haggling and begging and scheming over the pittance necessary to accept Liberty, the symbol of equality of all the citizens of the Republic. The dash of one millionaire's pen would have spared the city humiliation. None had come forward. Therefore the *World* would start its own campaign to finance the pedestal; it would receive all gifts, one dollar and up, and print the names of the donors in its columns.

A good attention-getter, the campaign, however, brought in little cash, and Pulitzer soon turned his energies to other, fresher causes.

In the fall of 1884, as the *Bartholdi* chugged across the bay and the gang of laborers dug the foundation, the grand total of some $125,000 collected from all sources sank steadily, as the account books showed all expenditure, no further income. Now was the time for

responsible government to come to the aid of all good men. The state legislature put through a bill allowing the city of New York to pay part of the cost; the governor vetoed it. The Congress also proved sticky. The House in the end refused to vote $100,000 for the project: it was a dangerous precedent to dip into the federal treasury for private purposes. The whole affair was by now embarrassing, which showed the danger of giving sentiment priority over practicality. The *Times* returned to the attack; the monument from France was just not useful.

Meanwhile the cases were being packed in Paris. What would be done with them if they actually arrived? To add to the humiliation, Boston and Baltimore — my God, even Minneapolis! — offered to do right by the copper lady.

In March 1885 Pulitzer returned to the fray. He now pointed out that it would be "an irrevocable disgrace to New York City and the American Republic to have France send us this splendid gift without our having provided even so much as a landing place for it." Recalling the ragged sufferers of Valley Forge and a century of amity, "the people's paper," the *World,* began a campaign directed at the masses. It had now discovered its audience and hammered away at it. Day after day, it printed pathetic little letters to show the sacrifices made for the cause.

Inclosed please find five cents as a poor office boy's mite toward the pedestal fund. As being loyal to the Stars and Stripes, I thought even five cents would be acceptable.

A lonely and very aged woman with very limited means wishes to add her mite to the Bartholdi fund. Hoping that the inclosed dollar may induce multitudes all over the country to respond and that the enterprise may be very speedily accomplished is the earnest wish of the writer.

I am a wee bit of a girl, yet I am ever so glad I was born in time to contribute my mite to the pedestal fund. When I am old enough I will ask my papa and mama to take me to see the statue, and I will always be proud that I began my career by sending you $1 to aid in so good a cause.

Who cared whether the letters were faked or not! They made good copy and sustained interest. The ceaseless reminders, the long lists of names, theatrical and sports benefits, all kept the issue alive for two months until the total was in. The number of subscribers rose to 120,000 and a good part of the total collected was contributed in amounts of $1.00 or less. The impact of accumulated little gifts achieved in a few weeks what years of dining and oratory had failed to accomplish.

The *Isère* arrived off Sandy Hook on the morning of May 17, 1885, and two days later the transfer of the precious cargo to Bedloe's Island began, before an audience of five thousand spectators crowded onto three ferries. The pedestal was now being hastily completed and the work of assembly got under way. Bartholdi appeared for a month in October to be sure the procedures were right, but there remained mostly the laborious job of fastening the pieces together with 300,000 copper rivets. Then, at last, the sculptor's vision had become a reality. Liberty towered above the bay, her 151-foot height sustained by a pedestal 89

The World.

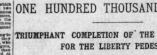

VOL. XXVI., NO. 8,757. NEW YORK, TUESDAY, AUGUST 11, 1885----WITH SUPPLEMENT. PRICE TWO CENTS.

THE SPECTRE IN GRANADA.

A CONDITION MORE HORRIBLE THAN THAT OF NAPLES LAST YEAR.

Cholera Victims Decaying in the Streets—Three Hundred Deaths in Marseilles—Missionaries Massacred by Black Flags in Tonquin—Fatal Fall of an English Railway Station Roof.

MADRID, Aug. 10.—Granada is to-day in a most desperate condition, as a result of the ravages of cholera. The state of affairs there is really worse than it was in Naples last year during the cholera epidemic in that city. There are no doctors now in Granada, and the dead bodies of cholera victims lie unburied in the streets. There were 4,711 new cases of cholera and 1,513 deaths from the disease reported yesterday throughout Spain.

MURDERED IN HIS HOME.

A WEALTHY BROOKLYNITE SHOT DOWN BY A HIDDEN FOE.

Albert R. Herrick, Whose Place of Business is at No. 60 William Street, this City, Dies Before He Can Tell Who Fired the Fatal Shot—The Police Without a Clue.

Mr. Albert R. Herrick, who keeps a restaurant at No. 60 William street, this city, was shot and killed yesterday under mysterious circumstances at his residence, No. 22 Pearl street, Brooklyn.

ONE HUNDRED THOUSAND DOLLARS!

TRIUMPHANT COMPLETION OF THE WORLD'S FUND FOR THE LIBERTY PEDESTAL.

Story of the Greatest Popular Subscription Ever Raised in America—How the Republic Was Saved from Lasting Disgrace—An Event for Patriotic Citizens to Rejoice Over—A Roll of Honor Bearing the Names of 120,000 Generous Patriots—The Flags of France and the American Union Floating in Sisterly Sympathy—Over $3,300 Received Yesterday—The Grand Total Foots Up $102,006.39—A Generous Lady Pays $130 for the Washington Cent.

THIS PEDESTAL TO LIBERTY WAS PROVIDED BY THE VOLUNTARY CONTRIBUTIONS OF 120,000 PATRIOTIC CITIZENS OF THE AMERICAN UNION THROUGH THE NEW YORK WORLD FINIS CORONAT OPUS

feet high, which in turn rested on a 65-foot base.

A final imbroglio before the great inauguration ceremony: clearly it was the responsibility of the federal government, which had accepted the monument, to pay for the cost of equipping and unveiling it. The suspicious congressmen were not sure and chewed over the issue for weeks before finally authorizing the expenditure of $56,000.

On October 28, 1886, President Grover Cleveland presided over the inauguration ceremony. Bartholdi was there, but Laboulaye had been dead for three years. Many other distinguished guests graced the occasion and listened to the speeches. A full complement of French dignitaries represented the Senate and the Chamber of Deputies as well as the more important ministries. On the American side, the secretaries of State, War, Navy, and Interior accompanied the president. A salute from all the batteries in the harbor, ashore and afloat, marked the final unveiling, timed to come near sunset. Then the torch was illuminated.

The little flame cast the light of a glowworm, complained Bartholdi, who had expected a tremendous flare.

The flame burned more intensely than he knew.

A thirty-three-year-old Cuban poet was then in New York, earning a living by writing articles for Latin American newspapers. Now he observed the enshrinement of Liberty; a few years later he would die fighting for the independence of his native land.

José Martí was not among the distinguished guests. He mingled with the crowd, saw not an empty spot on the streets along the way, saw the harbor dense with ships and the ships dense with passengers, saw the new Brooklyn Bridge thick with watchers. He felt the throb of popular excitement, sensed the flags flying in the hearts of men as well as from the roofs of buildings. A deep respect ennobled every thought, as if the arrival and erection of the statue called to mind all those who had died to win liberty.

A symbol could have many meanings. The press comments the next day reflected the diversity. For the *Mobile Register* the statue meant simply Franco-American friendship confirmed by free government. For the New York *World* and the *Pittsburgh Dispatch* it stood for vigilance against either oppressive privileges for wealth or the destructive disorders of a lawless proletariat. For the New York *Irish-American* it represented the continuing struggle against English feudalism. *L'Echo d'Italia* of New York emphasized the number of Italian societies that marched as groups in the grand parade. The *Augusta* (Georgia) *Chronicle* wondered whether a pagan divinity was really appropriate in a Christian country; and the *Times* of London snickered at the curious festival in which France, which had too little, exported Liberty to America, which had too much. Only the *New York Herald* commented on the huge steamship crowded with immigrants — who watched the wonderful drama as they passed — and wondered what the ceremony could have meant to their tired eyes.

Then and later there seemed a discrepancy between the notables who served on committees and made speeches and the onlookers who followed the parade and cheered the orators. For the former the monument was a nice gesture, betokening Franco-American

By 1883 Bartholdi's task was virtually complete, and the sculptor turned his attention westward — only to discover that the American team had fallen seriously behind schedule. Plagued by financial difficulties and ignored by an apathetic public, the statue's stateside sponsors had been able to erect less than a third of the pedestal, and the base itself — built upon the star-shaped foundation of an abandoned fort — was strewn with rubble (left). When the three-masted Isère *and its precious cargo of copper plate and iron bracing arrived in New York harbor in May 1885, the cheering throngs (below) that greeted Bartholdi's creation were obliged to hoist the tricolor over a still-unfinished pedestal.*

friendship and the ideas of the Enlightenment. In the benediction, the Reverend Richard S. Storrs gave praise for the kindly affection of one great nation toward another. Count Ferdinand de Lesseps extolled the virtues of "the country where the individual initiative is developed in all its powers; where progress is religion; where large fortunes become the property of the people," and reminded Americans that France had helped make them powerful and free. William M. Evarts reciprocated by extolling the liberty-loving people who had made the gift; and President Cleveland accepted the gift as a token of "the kinship of republics." This was "a pledge of fraternal union between the two greatest republics of the world," said French minister W. A. Lefaivre. And Chauncey M. Depew's culminating oration touched on Lafayette, Washington, and the blood of our fathers commingling upon the battlefields of the Revolution in a final splash of rhetoric. The venerable poet John Greenleaf Whittier expressed all these official sentiments in a style that even then appeared antique:

> O France, the beautiful! to thee
>   Once more a debt of love we owe:
> In peace beneath thy fleur-de-lis,
>   We hail a later Rochambeau!
>
> Shine far, shine free, a guiding light
>   To Reason's ways and Virtue's aim,
> A lightening-flash the wretch to smite
>   Who shields his license with thy name!

The lines rhymed, the spelling and grammar were good. The poem was dead.

And so too were the feelings of distinguished people

Three weeks before the formal unveiling, workmen were still swarming over Eiffel's iron skeleton. The engravings at left, both of which appeared in Frank Leslie's Illustrated Newspaper *in October 1886, show the final stages of assembly. In the top view the armatures for the head and torch are readied; below, inside the head, plates forming the statue's face are riveted into place beneath the slotted tiara. Artist Edward Moran's depiction of the unveiling (right) shows Liberty banked by massed flags and shrouded in smoke from the muzzles of countless ships' guns.*

about the statue. Tourists and foreigners went to see it; but the government was perfunctory in its custody. Money was never adequate and the responsibility for the monument long fell on the Lighthouse Bureau, in accord with the fiction that the torch was an aid to navigation. Conscientious though the officials might be, this structure was not within their competence or their concern.

But for millions who first saw the upraised torch from the steerage of ships coming through the narrows, the statue had a different meaning, one that also attracted millions of native-born men and women, who had learned the significance of their country's history by experience.

The New World had always been a place of refuge, for the victims of religious persecution, for the rebels against oppressive government, and for the depressed populations of lands without opportunity. For such people, liberty was not an abstraction, it was the life-giving shelter that gave them air to breath. Mangold, a local poet, put it simply in the dialect of Bartholdi's Colmar:

> *Amerika, uf alle Flanke*
> *Bésch du fo's wahre Züefluchtsland.*
> *Eurral gét's Volker wo noch Zanke,*
> *Wàm reich sie enander d' Hand?*

America, in every latitude you are the true land of refuge. Wherever people still struggle, to whom do they stretch their hand?

There was little official recognition, however, of this popular meaning ascribed to the statue. Only after the turn of the century was the connection established

between the monument and the massive flow of immigrants who landed at nearby Ellis Island. In 1903 a bronze plaque affixed to the statue permanently made the association. The plaque carried a simple poem, "The New Colossus," which had originally appeared in a collection that accompanied an art exhibition to aid the fund gathering back in 1883. It had attracted little attention at the time.

Its author was Emma Lazarus, by then a practiced poet, although this theme was somewhat outside her usual line. Emma had lived a sheltered life. The daughter of a wealthy Jewish family prominent in New York since colonial times, she had been a girl of sensibility and early in life had begun to put her feelings into verse. Her model was Ralph Waldo Emerson and though she was somewhat disappointed when she finally met the great man, the influence of his transcendentalist ideas upon her endured through life. Communion with nature, a vague mystical yearning, and an undefined faith gave her writing a somewhat ethereal quality. "The New Colossus" was quite a different kind of work.

The words breathed passion. The message was direct. Liberty's name was Mother of Exiles and she spoke with silent lips. Disdaining the pomp of ancient lands, she cried:

> Give me your tired, your poor,
> Your huddled masses yearning to breathe free,
> The wretched refuse of your teeming shore.
> Send these, the homeless, tempest-tost to me,
> I lift my lamp beside the golden door!

When he read those lines, James Russell Lowell, a fastidious critic, wrote that the poem gave the statue a

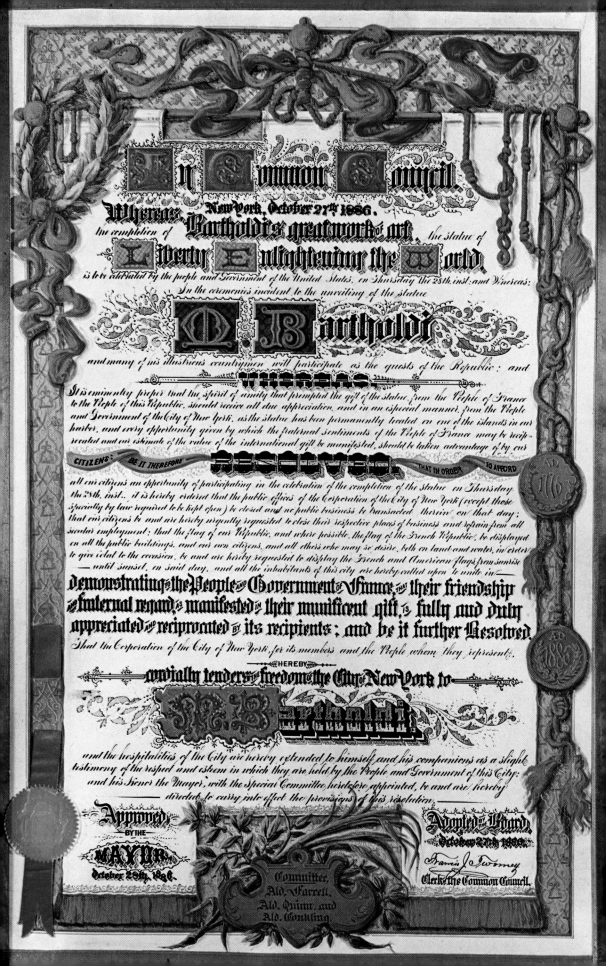

The effusion of goodwill that attended Liberty's unveiling was genuine if overblown, and there can be little doubt that the special proclamation at left — which cites the people and the government of France for their "munificent gift" — was tendered sincerely. That extravagantly illuminated document welcomes Bartholdi's "great work of art" to New York and proffers the "Freedom of the City" to the sculptor himself. Tiffany's commemorated the event in its own fashion (below) — with an ornate silver orb surmounted by an arm and torch and resting on a base of polished petrified wood emblazoned with a silver bas-relief of the statue itself.

raison d'être which it had previously lacked, quite as much as it had then lacked a pedestal.

The shock of remote events in Russia had broken the crust of genteel sentiment that until then had guarded the sheltered young woman's emotions. Emma Lazarus had little in common with the Jews who lived a traditional life in the distant and secluded villages of Eastern Europe. But the wave of pogroms that spread through the tsar's dominions horrified Americans of every faith. Ex-President Grant and William M. Evarts were among those who expressed outrage at the retrogression to a barbarism that ran counter to the spirit of the age. As the news of persecution flowed in, Emma felt the stirring of a deeper sentiment than had ever moved her before.

The first literary expression of her reaction came in prose. In the *Century Magazine* of April 1882, Madame Ragozin, a Russian lady of quality, defended her countrymen; certainly the excesses were too much, but they were understandable because the Jews were an alien, backward lump in society, cruelly exploiting the peasants. Emma Lazarus responded. She knew little about conditions in Eastern Europe and lacked the factual information with which to defend her coreligionists. But she had a sense of the sweep of their tragic history and vaguely felt the power of the faith to which they held after centuries of tribulation. The certainty of God's presence in the world, which was the rock on which they stood, she identified with her own (and Emerson's) mystical certainty of a Divine presence. That certainty had once spoken through the mouths of the prophets. "The Spirit is not dead," she insisted, "proclaim the word."

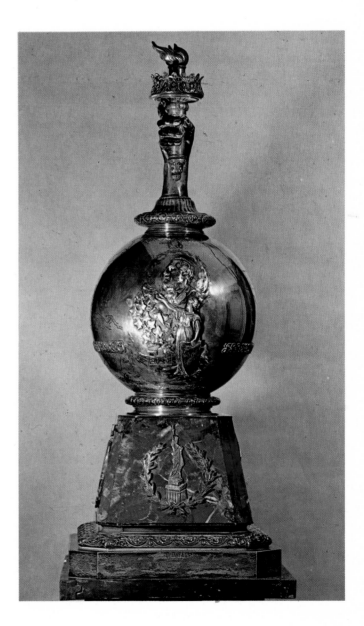

This literary gesture drew Emma into unfamiliar activities. She became involved in efforts to aid the fugitives from Russian tyranny. And now she met, among the fugitives, men of talent and accomplishment who were gratefully engaged in menial labor for the sake of the freedom she and other Americans accepted so casually.

When the request came for a poem on the statue, she was at first cool; a sensitive artist did not produce to order. Then the words poured forth from her heart.

"The New Colossus" at first gained little attention except from readers like Lowell who recognized its poetic worth. Whittier's lines, not those of Emma Lazarus, appeared at the dedication ceremony. Not until two decades later did her statement earn widespread recognition.

In 1883 the greatest wave of immigration was only beginning. In 1903 it was at full tide. The newcomers numbered in the millions and they came from every corner of Europe. They created grave problems. But they also vividly brought to the attention of Americans the meaning liberty had to humble people far from the shores of the United States.

Gradually thereafter the awareness spread not only of the significance of the lines of the poem but also of the significance of the aspect of national tradition it expressed. Liberty was not simply the bond between ancient allies; nor was it only the symbol of liberal ideas of justice and freedom; it was also the motive force that had peopled the wilderness and made the country that emerged what it was.

In the twentieth century, there were repeated occasions for re-examining the past and wondering whether old traditions that had worked so well still had value.

On December 2, 1916, President Woodrow Wilson came to Bedloe's Island. The statue had been refurbished that year and he was to inaugurate a new lighting system. The concerns of one term in office weighed heavily upon him and he had just narrowly come through a grueling election campaign. The cruel war in Europe also worried him, for he doubted that his country would escape involvement and he knew what costs that would entail. But he was also aware of the nation's doubts about itself; the year before he had vetoed, and the next year he would see passed over another veto, a law designed to exclude any new immigrants from southern and eastern Europe, a sharp break with earlier tradition. Trained as a historian, he knew the past meaning of the free movement of peoples, and the demands for change troubled him.

Twenty years went by. Bartholdi's statue became a national monument in 1924, first under the charge of the War Department, then after 1933 under the National Park Service of the Department of the Interior. In 1931 it once more acquired a new lighting system. But despite the prosperity of the 1920's, Wilson's forebodings were not unfounded. An uncertain nation closed its gates to newcomers by a law enacted ironically in 1924, the same year in which Liberty became a monument and ceased to be Mother of Exiles. A great Red scare at home severely restrained freedom of expression, and in 1929 began the long agony of economic depression that left millions in want.

The fiftieth anniversary of the dedication fell in 1936, again during a divisive national election, again at a moment of impending crisis. President Franklin

Two years before the crated statue arrived in New York its spirit affected a young Jewish poetess named Emma Lazarus (left) so deeply that she felt compelled to express her feelings in verse. Over the years the closing lines of "The New Colossus" were to become almost as well known as the statue to which they were ultimately affixed. For oppressed peoples in all parts of the globe, the words that Emma Lazarus had penned in 1883 (far left) were inextricably associated with the monument that Bartholdi had conceived. The statue itself rapidly became a phenomenally popular tourist attraction, as Frank Leslie's Illustrated Newspaper *accurately predicted when it published the fanciful view below a year before the statue was finally erected.*

Delano Roosevelt came to mark the occasion. Of course New York was an important state and the immigrants and their children were significant elements in his following. Still he did not deliver a thumping campaign speech. Instead, he took a long view of the significance of the statue and, though an amateur, he was enough of a historian to appreciate its place in the national past, its possible meaning for the future. His address drew together the vision, inherited from the European Enlightenment, of America as the home of liberty and the popular dream of America as the land of promise.

America was mankind's second chance, withheld by the Almighty until men most needed liberty and were enlightened enough to establish it on foundations sound enough to maintain it. For over three centuries a steady stream of men, women, and children followed the beacon of liberty that the light symbolized. They adopted the new homeland because it offered them the things they most desired — freedom of opportunity, freedom of thought, freedom to worship God as they wished. "Here they found life because here there was freedom to live."

The president's thoughts turned to the millions who came in steerage and saw in the strange horizon visions denied to the eyes of the few who traveled in greater luxury. The universal language of human aspiration brought them to the New World and their effort and devotion made its freedom safer, richer, more far-reaching, and more capable of growth than before. The realization that all were bound together by hope of a common future rather than by reverence for a common past helped build upon this continent a unity of general purpose unapproached in the world. The decade that followed would severely test that unity.

A quarter-century after F.D.R. spoke, a new young president was learning the burdens that came with the White House. Aware of his own Irish Catholic heritage, John F. Kennedy had written *A Nation of Immigrants,* an appreciative book about the variety of peoples who had formed the American nation. His interest helped to bring to fulfillment a languishing project to house an immigration museum on Bedloe's Island.

Bartholdi's monument had used only part of the island's twelve acres. The base, pedestal, and statue all stood within the thick walls of a land battery built between 1806 and 1811 to defend New York against naval attack. The military installation, in the form of an eleven-point star, was later called Fort Wood and served as an artillery garrison, ordinance depot, recruiting center, and quarantine station. But the post, never very useful, had gradually fallen into decay, and it had been abandoned in 1877. There had been no objection to its use as the site of the monument. The recurrent projects for refurbishing the statue had resulted in a rebuilding of the walls, and a general cleaning up of the area, but the space had never been put to any purposeful use.

World War II and the uncertain peace that followed found the foreign-born citizens and their children unswervingly loyal. The men in the ranks who bore German or Italian or Japanese names proved not to be confused as to which was their country and which the enemy's and proved capable also of seeing through the Fascist and Communist conspiracies against democracy. In civilian life, moreover, their talents and labors contributed to the welfare of all. Above all, the United States had learned something before Kennedy's time of the necessity of cooperation without loss of freedom.

It was altogether fitting therefore that a group of citizens should have united in the 1950's to create a new museum to commemorate the contributions of immigrants to American life to be housed at the base of the Statue of Liberty. The roster of the national committee that launched a fund drive in 1956 was itself expressive. U. S. Grant III and Alexander Hamilton, Pierre S. du Pont III and Spyros Skouras, Theodore Blegen and Sou Chan, Yaroslav Chyz and Edward Corsi, George Meany and William Rosenwald were all Americans. At whatever date their forebears reached the New World, all had been strangers in the land, and all had shared and participated in the common experience of creating its culture.

A question persisted through the 1960's, however. Would the experience of drawing different people together and uniting them in liberty remain something to be symbolized and venerated in monuments and museums or would it cast light along the hazardous way as Americans moved toward a perilous future?

IV

RELIGIOUS LIBERTY

Bartholdi faced the simple problem: how to give the idea of liberty a form in metal. The Americans who contributed to the pedestal considered a more complex issue: what had liberty meant in their national experience? But the question that concerned millions of immigrants who peopled the United States was most difficult of all: what way of life could people live in liberty?

The question was not at all theoretical. Upon the answer hung the practical decisions that took thousands of families and individuals on hazardous adventures to a strange new world. Yet the great majority of those who came were unprepared to grasp the meaning of liberty. Certainly many longed for relief from the burdens that law, custom, and economic deprivation had forced upon them. But few could imagine an existence without restraint; just as prisoners grown familiar with the routine of the cells — while continuing to dream of release — are unable to conceive of a society in which men can act without the guidance of bars and patrolled corridors.

The possibilities of freedom dawned slowly: at first upon a few driven by the claims of conscience, then upon the greater crowd of fugitives who wished to escape from political oppression, and finally upon the masses who fled from poverty. In time the host swelled, sweeping along men and women from every corner of the earth for whom America had become the land of liberty.

During the years Bartholdi's project was taking form, the contrast that seemed most striking in European eyes was that between the religious liberty Americans enjoyed and the bitter controversies that still disturbed the Old World. None of the European nations in the

A foreshortened view of the Statue of Liberty

nineteenth century had yet resolved the issue of Church and State. Britain, which was closest to the United States in the matter, still supported an established church and put dissenters at a disadvantage. Russia always subjected nonbelievers to discrimination and sometimes to violence. The other countries fell somewhere between.

America had escaped these difficulties. "This whole vast chapter of debate and stress," which had caused half the wars, half the internal strife of Europe, remained unwritten in the United States where all religious bodies were absolutely equal before the law and recognized only as voluntary associations of private citizens. That was the judgment in 1885 of Viscount James Bryce, an informed Scotsman who knew America well.

Yet religious freedom in its modern form was an unforeseen by-product of the circumstances of settlement. The seventeenth-century colonists did not bring with them any such full-fledged theory. Nor did the liberty of each person to worship as he wished develop deliberately through legislation. It emerged rather as the unplanned response to the conditions under which men and women peopled the wilderness.

Their relations to God were of the utmost importance to the first settlers. Faith informed them of the correct doctrines and the oversight of the organized church assured correct behavior. Each person knew that he was a player in a divine drama that began with the Creation and would end some day with the Redemption of the universe. Central to the plot of the drama was the fate of the immortal soul which, tested in the brief span of earthly experience, would earn either the reward of heavenly bliss or the punishment

of eternal damnation. The devout, absolutely convinced of the rightness of their views, felt no obligation to tolerate dissent, which was the same as encouraging error and might lead the innocent into sin. Better to extirpate heresy in the flames that burned about the stakes of innumerable execution places than to risk forever the tender souls of the fallible multitude.

The earliest colonists brought to America the same attitude about religion they had held in Europe. The truth was one and indivisible, known through the established church and supported by state power. Heresy was a dangerous trap set by Satan to mislead the unwary; the righteous priest would condemn it and the righteous magistrate would punish it. The torture chamber and the edict of banishment were appropriate means of safeguarding souls for eternity. So for hundreds of years men had fought one another in the name of a jealous God; and the voyage across the Atlantic did not in the least diminish the zeal for persecution.

Tolerance did not spring full grown from the soil of the New World. The Puritans left England for the Massachusetts Bay Colony for the sake of freedom—that is, of their own freedom to join in purified churches and to worship in a holy manner, without the danger from contamination that abounded in the corruptions of England. To assure their own liberty they intended to found a commonwealth guided by the precepts of the Bible. But they had no intention of extending the same liberty to those who disagreed with them — that is, to those who were wrong. When Anne Hutchinson began to preach in an unorthodox fashion, the Puritans sternly drove her away lest her disruptive ideals cloud what they knew to be the truth and threaten

everyone in the community with eternal damnation.

With regard to religious tolerance America was different from Europe in only one respect. In America there was space. Anne Hutchinson, driven from Massachusetts, moved to Rhode Island and there worshiped in her own fashion. The tiny settlements along the coast were lost in a vast emptiness, and people not tolerated in one place could make homes in another. Furthermore, English colonization was neither as centralized nor as orderly as that conducted by the French or Spaniards. The English planted themselves in America in a series of unconnected stabs at the coastline, each under different auspices, and each often with a different variety of faith — the Church of England in Virginia, Roman Catholics in Maryland, Separatists in Plymouth, and Puritans in Massachusetts; and provinces captured from the Dutch added to the diversity. No theory as yet explained or justified the situation, but in practice during the seventeenth century, the American wilderness came to shelter men of substantially dissimilar faiths.

Gradually, the colonists learned to live with a condition that many still regarded as disorderly and regrettable. It would have been better had every resident been a communicant of the same church, but for the time being there were advantages to tolerating people of all faiths. Land, the sole resource the society possessed, gained value only with hands to work it; and in the struggle for survival and expansion the willingness to labor began to seem more important than adherence to one creed rather than another.

Slowly theory and institutions caught up with this reality. A godly young minister, among the early arrivals in Massachusetts, started voicing doubts about all links between Church and State, between faith and power. Descended from a good family, a graduate of Cambridge and pious in his external life, Roger Williams could have had his choice of pulpits in the Puritan colony. But he believed that religious obedience was due only to God speaking through the promptings of the individual conscience, that inner faculty through which men recognized His voice. Himself always a seeker after truth, Williams opposed any effort to force others to assent to doctrines they would not willingly accept. It followed therefore that a good society ought to require no test of faith of its residents. He went south from Boston to Rhode Island, where he was instrumental in setting up a government that tolerated every variety of worship.

The idea of admitting settlers without regard to religious qualifications took hold because it conformed to the needs of the sparsely populated settlements. In 1658 the people of Flushing in New Netherland remonstrated against a proposed law curbing the Quakers. After all, the complaint explained, even Jews, Turks, and Egyptians were the sons of Adam. Love, peace, and liberty therefore were to extend to everyone so that hatred, war, and bondage might soon disappear. "Our desire is to do unto all men as we desire all men should do unto us, which is the true law both of Church and State." That simple proposition gained in persuasiveness as the decades passed.

The old discriminatory statutes remained on the books, but the law nevertheless changed subtly and the pressure to adjust the rules to the new conditions reached the king himself. Charles II became aware of

the situation soon after his restoration to the throne of England in 1661. The country had passed through decades of violent revolution in the course of which his royal father had lost both crown and head; Charles returned from exile determined to restore order, uniformity, and the authority of the established church. But he found it awkward to insist upon the same standards for the colonies, which already sheltered religious dissenters and which might in the future gain more population by a lax than by a rigid policy.

Charles and his ministers faced the issue squarely when called on to grant a new charter to Rhode Island. That colony had long been totally permissive about religion and insisted upon recognition of its unorthodox practice. The king yielded. The charter noted that within England itself uniformity was necessary, but that, by reason of its remote distance, the colony deserved a concession. Therefore the charter provided that no person at any time was in any way to be molested, punished, disquieted, or called into question for any differences of opinion in matters of religion as long as he did not actually disturb the civil peace. Furthermore, no future law nor any existing custom could alter the rights bestowed. The people of Rhode Island thus acquired a liberty far broader than that of the mother country.

At about the same time the Dutch West India Company confessed that it could not proceed against nonbelievers in New Amsterdam as rigorously as it wished. It feared that strict laws would diminish the population and stop immigration, which was still essential to the country's existence. It therefore instructed the governor of New Netherland: "shut your eyes!"

Do not "force people's consciences, but allow every one to have his own belief, as long as he behaves quietly and legally, gives no offense to his neighbors and does not oppose the government." The desire to draw settlers to their empty lands justified similar concessions by the Carolina proprietors. The right of residence in the colonies thus extended to people who did not conform to the dominant faith while such tolerance of nonconformity was still a distant ideal in Europe.

The best-known experiment with religious liberty was the outcome of the experience of the Quakers. The Society of Friends took form in the 1650's under the leadership of George Fox. A seeker after the truth like Roger Williams, Fox was dissatisfied with the answers the existing churches gave. Searching the promptings of his own heart, he argued that all men ought to follow the guidance of the Inner Light, which directly inspired each of them. These views spread not simply because of the eloquence of the preacher, but also because they satisfied the needs of many troubled people. The times were disturbed and society all topsy-turvy, with no king to give it order and all institutions being challenged. Men tired of fighting, and weary of endless theological disputes, eagerly seized upon a doctrine attractive in its utter simplicity. All the disputes of the previous century became irrelevant by the new formula: no priests, no sacraments, no ritual, no oaths, no deference. The enthusiastic adherents, eager to win converts, carried the message throughout the realm with unrestrained zeal. Outlandish in dress and mode of speech, they respected no conventional customs and did not hesitate to offend others as a way of winning attention. And they willingly accepted punishment

as a means of bearing witness to their faith.

The subversive behavior of the Quakers antagonized the authorities everywhere, but particularly in the colonies, where the law was precarious and challenges to it might lead to anarchy and destroy the very foundation of society. Ruthless persecution was the response to the appearance of the Quakers in America. The tolerance extended to others was not for them; most provinces summarily ordered them to leave; and Massachusetts in 1661 executed four especially contumacious Friends.

After 1670, the sect became somewhat more respectable, made influential converts, and adopted quieter techniques of persuasion. Its members lost the old eagerness to be missionaries and began to concentrate upon leading their own way of life, neither interfering with, nor suffering interference from, others. The obligation to go forth to disturb the world now seemed less important than the opportunity to withdraw to a place where they could conduct themselves without offense in their own manner. A Friend named John Archdale in 1678 purchased part of the proprietary rights to Carolina in the hope of providing such a refuge.

His plan bore no fruit. Instead, the Delaware Valley became the site of the Quaker experiment and William Penn, its chief promoter. Penn's father, a fighting man, rose to high rank under Cromwell, but at the Restoration he promptly transferred his loyalty to Charles II and thrived under the monarchy as he had under the Commonwealth. The younger Penn studied at Oxford, traveled on the Continent and was ready for a gentleman's career when he fell under the influence of the

Quakers. Twice imprisoned for his beliefs, William Penn labored as a missionary in Germany and soon became involved in plans to create a colony of Friends in America. He first took part in a project already under way to develop West New Jersey. A group of well-to-do Quakers from England and Ireland had begun to send settlers across in 1675 and succeeded in arranging the move of some 1,700 of their coreligionists in the next seven years.

Penn, impatient with what he considered slow growth and discontent with the uncertainties of the Jersey title, proceeded to launch a larger scheme across the Delaware River. Pennsylvania grew with phenomenal rapidity. In 1683 it received 3,000 settlers. Five years later its population had risen to 12,000, for it proved attractive to Friends from Germany and Holland as well as those from England and Ireland. But Pennsylvania did not become solely a society of Quakers. Rather it welcomed every sort of "plain and well-intending people," ready to work to develop the country. It therefore operated on a basis like that of Rhode Island, tolerating all sects.

The practical necessities of settlement forced all the colonies in the same general direction. Each developed its own pattern of relations between Church and State: some supporting favored sects with the proceeds of taxes, others not; some permitting all forms of public worship, others not; some extending full civic rights to the unorthodox, others discriminating against them when it came to voting or officeholding. But everywhere in America the dissenting stranger was free to live in peace.

The colonies therefore became a magnet that at-

The installation of 600 shards of tinted cathedral glass in place of Bartholdi's original copper sheeting has heightened the lighting effects of the beacon of liberty.

tracted the victims of European persecution. In 1685, for instance, the French government revoked the Edict of Nantes, which had allowed the Huguenots to live in the country despite their Protestantism. Those who stubbornly clung to their faith departed, many of them to the New World where their skill and capital earned them respected places in communities along the coast from South Carolina to Massachusetts.

At about the same time, persecuted covenanters in the Scottish Lowlands also proposed to establish a colony in Carolina. With the support of Lord Cardross one hundred of them established a settlement at Port Royal. They hoped that as many as ten thousand others would follow. But the Spaniards wiped out the pioneers and there were no followers.

Before the seventeenth century was over, however, the promotional tracts spread by Penn and others on the continent of Europe began to draw a flow of newcomers seeking religious freedom. It was not surprising that a substantial number of German Quakers settled near Philadelphia in Germantown, which Francis Daniel Pastorius had laid out for them. More significant was the welcome accorded the group of Anabaptists who called themselves Mennonites after a sixteenth-century Dutch reformer and who also located themselves in Pennsylvania. Guiding their lives by a strict reading of the Bible and avoiding all worldly affairs, they formed tight congregations that retained their distinctiveness generation after generation. Indeed, the worldliness of some caused one group, the Amish, to split away into a sect of their own, which outdid the rest in maintaining its distance from other Americans.

Pennsylvania became home to other German sects also. In the 1730's Johann Conrad Beissel established the Ephrata Cloisters, near Lancaster. There the Dunkards formed a communal order that was dedicated to labor and to music. A decade later, Count Nikolaus Ludwig von Zinzendorf established a settlement of Moravians in Bethlehem, Pennsylvania. For centuries, the members of this community had kept their faith alive in Central Europe under conditions of great difficulty. In Pennsylvania and North Carolina, they found space in the 1740's to lead their lives in their own way without interference.

In 1774 Mother Ann Lee arrived in New England from old England along with a small group of her Shaker followers. Their views were remote from those of the people among whom they resided. The United Society of Believers in Christ's Second Appearing, as they called themselves, held that God had revealed himself in Christ as the male, and in Mother Ann as the female, principle. The Shakers were celibate, held property in common, and worked and lived cooperatively. Later they refused to perform military service or to acknowledge the authority of government. Nevertheless they settled in peace and rarely encountered hostility from their unconverted neighbors. The same tolerance accorded them extended as readily to individuals and groups whose differences with the majority were less extreme.

By the revolutionary era, however, tolerance was no longer enough; the mixture of populations and creeds had created a condition that called for more — for equality. Men of different faiths worked together in creating a society. Why should some modes of worship be more privileged than others? Religious affiliation bore no re-

lationship relevant to people's ability to cooperate or to the usefulness of their contributions to the national welfare. All therefore deserved to be on an equal footing in the eyes of the law.

The heritage of establishment stood in the way. Some churches received support from taxes while others did not; and in some places a religious test remained a qualification for voting or holding office. In practice the colonies made efforts to soften the effect of the law through compromise or evasion. The old religious forms dissolved only when the Revolution severed all ties with Britain. After 1776, establishment seemed a relic of monarchy and of dependence on England, and therefore inappropriate to the new republic. Furthermore, among the patriots were Catholics, Jews, and Deists, as well as Protestants of many sects. It was invidious to discriminate among them when the time came to enjoy the liberty for which all had fought.

The temper of the revolutionary era received most eloquent expression in the Virginia law to establish religious equality. The Bill of Rights of that state in 1776, much copied elsewhere, had already gone far in proclaiming that only reason and conviction, not force or violence, could direct the manner of discharging the duty owed to the Creator. All men were therefore equally entitled to the free exercise of religion according to the dictates of conscience, and it was the mutual duty of all to practice Christian forebearance, love, and charity toward each other.

This guarantee of tolerance for all was a considerable step toward religious liberty. It gave permanence to the advances of the previous century. But it did not move far enough forward for the tastes of Thomas Jefferson

A cluster of high-intensity incandescent lamps gives Liberty's torch the equivalent of 2,500 times the brightness of full moonlight. Engineers servicing this complex electrical system must mount the metal rungs of a steep ladder within the statue's upraised arm to reach the 1,000-watt bulbs seen in the close-up at left. The bright red and yellow tinted glass of the flame's tip is visible above the lamps.

or James Madison, for it left open the possibility that the government might still interfere in matters of faith without penalizing the members of any specific sect. In 1786, therefore, they persuaded the Virginia legislature to declare that all men possessed the natural right to profess whatever religion they wished or none and thereby to forbid any meddling at all with religion. They thus erected a wall of separation between Church and State. Five years later, the First Amendment to the Federal Constitution prohibited Congress from making any law with respect to religion.

By the end of the eighteenth century, the United States was so far ahead of any other nation in this respect that it offered a beacon of hope to those who suffered for their faith everywhere. Furthermore, the area of freedom widened steadily as other states, following the lead of Virginia, struck down inherited discriminatory practices. North Carolina, for instance, required officeholders to take an oath affirming the divine character of the New Testament; but a Jew who refused to do so in 1809 nevertheless was seated in the legislature. In 1826, Maryland eliminated from its constitution the similar requirement that officials declare their belief in the Christian religion. The leader of the fight for a change in Maryland was Thomas Kennedy, a Scotch Presbyterian immigrant and a member of the legislature whose interests in the issue were purely altruistic, for neither he nor his constituents were adversely affected by the offensive provisions. But the separation of Church and State, he believed, was among the proudest achievements of the Republic. "America," he said, "had forever sundered the spiritual from the temporal concerns of men"; and had left

it to backward monarchies to prop up faith by force.

The contrast between the freedom of the New World and the repression of the Old affected many groups. The Catholics, who were victims in Ireland of social prejudice and barred for a long time from full participation in politics, learned to look westward for asylum as did the Jews of continental Europe and other smaller groups, for whom religious freedom was a distant aspiration.

Changes in the law did not immediately eradicate prejudices held for centuries. But the assertion in the statutes that freedom and equality were the norms allowed strangers to live side by side and to get to know one another. In time, they could weigh the similarities that united them against the differences that divided them.

Boston, the Puritan capital, was by no means free of the old fear of papists in 1796. As a regular matter, the Harvard Dudlean lecturer denounced the wickedness of Rome while small boys played at persecution in the Common. That year the town nevertheless received a French clergyman, the Reverend Jean Louis Lefebvre de Cheverus, who was in time to become its first Catholic bishop. Although the Yankees slowly learned to tolerate him, his position was still not secure ten years later, when a call for solace drew him to the western part of the state. In Northampton, a jury had just condemned to death two Irishmen accused of murder. Father Cheverus insisted on preaching in the austere Congregational church of the town before the execution. He took as his text the sentence from John (I, 3:15), "Everyone who hates his brother is a murderer, and you know that no murderer has eternal life abid-

79

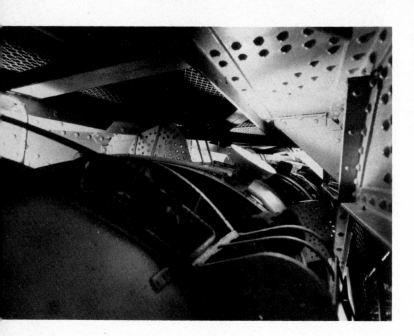

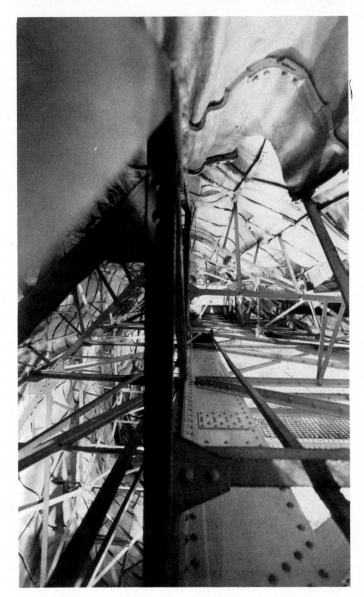

ing in him." His words, his presence, and his character had a remarkable impact on the townsfolk. Puzzled, Mrs. Mary Shepherd commented in her diary on this remarkable mild man who explained his religion in a very different manner from what she had always been taught. By the time he returned to France in 1823, he had acquired a glowing reputation for the sublime example of Christian virtue he offered his neighbors. "Who among our religious teachers would solicit a comparison between himself and the devoted Cheverus?" asked the Unitarian minister William Ellery Channing.

In the nineteenth century the principle of religious liberty and equality ceased to be abstract; living examples of the coexistence of different creeds made it a part of American life. The expanding nation became accustomed to the appearance of strangers who worshiped in their own ways; and the reputation for tolerance, spreading throughout Europe, attracted a multitude of dissenters of all sorts.

Southwest Germany furnished fertile soil for the sprouting of religious sects. Rival armies had time and again ravaged the land; and the desperate peasants gratefully turned to any messiah who offered them hope of relief. Johann Georg Rapp, one of those who urged a return to primitive Christian communism, in 1803 led a band of six hundred first to Harmony, Pennsylvania, and then to New Harmony, Indiana. The thriving community gave total obedience to its leader, practiced celibacy, and accepted the obligations of cooperative labor. Similar groups from Germany appeared in Zoar, Ohio, Bethel, Missouri, and Aurora, Oregon.

Faith also moved some Scandinavians to emigrate. So it was that Cleng Peerson, a Norwegian Quaker,

Two 168-step stairways — one for ascending, the other for descending — begin at the base of the statue and wind about a central column to the observation room in the crown. Weary tourists who pause at one of the numerous rest stations are often as astounded by the intricacy of the interior contours and construction as they are by the view of New York from the top.

came in 1821, spying out the land for those who professed his faith and suffered from intolerance at home. His report was encouraging enough to convince fifty of his fellows to take ship in the *Restauration,* a tiny vessel of thirty-eight tons that brought them to New York City. They settled near Rochester and they in turn sent back news that persuaded a second contingent to go forth to the Fox River settlement in Illinois. In time the followers of the Pietist Hans Nilsen Hauge and other dissenters also left Norway for American destinations.

So too a peasant prophet in Sweden looked to the United States for his promised land. Eric Janson was unlearned, sincere, emotional. His visions of a new life free of formal restraints cast a dazzling spell among a widening circle of his countrymen; four hundred of them came with him in 1846 to Bishop Hill, Illinois, and in time more than a thousand others joined them. They found shelter against the Midwest climate in caves scooped out of the earth and suffered tormenting hardships until 1848 when the first brick dormitories were finished. A year later cholera struck the young settlement a cruel blow. But tribulations such as these were tolerable, as long as the believers prayed together twice daily through the week and three times on Sunday and as long as they shared all their possessions. It was love that introduced the first note of discord, the love of John Root, a Stockholm man whom Janson refused to accept as his niece's husband. In 1850 the spurned suitor shot the prophet and although the community grew under Jonas Olson, who then assumed the leadership, it missed the authoritative judgment of its founder and dissolved in 1861.

The group that endured longest was the Community of the True Inspiration. The tradition accepted by its members traced its origins back to the sixteenth century, but it became visible as a religious order shortly after the end of the Napoleonic Wars in the battle-ravaged borderlands between France and Germany. The sect's leaders were all humble people—a tailor, a carpenter, and a peasant girl. They practiced communism and abjured all oaths, military service, and formal church organization, insisting that only through inspiration could the voice of God be heard. One such divine communication instructed them in 1826 to leave the places of their birth and to transfer themselves to the United States. But money for the move was not within easy reach of the poor. For sixteen years the community saved until it had the means in 1842 to purchase 5,000 acres near Buffalo. The settlement thrived, held together as it was by faith and devotion; and in 1854 when it was cramped for space began a further move to Amana, Iowa, where in time seven villages extended across 26,000 acres of productive farm land.

Outlandish as these groups seemed, other Americans rarely resented their arrival. After all, the country had space enough for everyone. And in any case, set off as they were in their own communities, the exotic religious groups were no threat to the values or habits of the majority. Nor, later, did the appearance of sizable contingents of Armenians cause any difficulty. These people carried with them a strange culture, Eastern in character, and they remained a group apart. Yet partly because they attracted sympathy as the victims of oppression and partly because some of them came under

the auspices of Protestant missionaries, the Armenians rarely met hostility, and they made places for themselves with equal readiness in the factories of Massachusetts and the farms of California.

It was quite another matter when the immigrants numbered in the millions and were not Protestants or even Christians.

The 1840's saw the beginning of an unprecedented mass migration. Hundreds of thousands of Irish Catholics arrived at the Atlantic seaports and settled not in remote isolation but in the hearts of the great cities. Later, substantial groups of Italians and Poles added to the number of communicants with Rome. Their appearance revived ancient fears and suspicions. They were foreign not only in birth, but perhaps also in the spiritual allegiance they owed the pope, who had long been reputed a foe of liberty and who, it was believed, only awaited the proper moment to summon up the forces of subversion to destroy the Republic. Who could tell what strange plots the alien clergy hatched in their secret nunneries and monasteries? It was all very well to tolerate a few cultivated men like Father Cheverus. But doubts welled up as to whether hundreds of thousands of priest-ridden Catholics could ever fully become Americans.

Well before this uneasiness subsided another exotic religious group made a claim for refuge. It had been easy enough to concede equality to the handful of Jews in eighteenth-century America. But after the 1850's the number grew, as the persecuted and poor spilled out of the ghettos of Germany and the little villages of Eastern Europe. The persecution of these people had always evoked sympathy in the United States; it was a relic of the backwardness of the Old World. But the attitude was somewhat qualified when thousands arrived, visible always in their strangeness whether peddling along the rural roads or thronging the slums of New York.

There was concern about them too. Age-old doubts about the people condemned to wander for having rejected the Savior, distaste for the killers of Christ, and disapproval of the usurers whose romantic destiny seemed tinged with magic disturbed many an American.

The arrival of the Catholics and Jews coincided with a dynamic resurgence of evangelical Protestantism in the United States. From hundreds of pulpits the call went forth: redeem the world, make the earth perfect. Earnest men and women labored to reform one another, to free the slaves, correct the criminals, heal the sick, and sober the drunkards. When moral exhortation proved inadequate, the reformers called upon the power of the state to eradicate evil by force of law. Often that involved an effort to legislate a specifically Protestant code of ethics as if that code should be binding on everyone.

The result was a running series of conflicts about issues that on the surface seemed petty yet which involved genuine divergences in fundamental points of view. Such, for instance, were the blue laws — which called for observance of the Puritan Sabbath—and prohibition. The dominant majority believed that these measures enlarged rather than narrowed liberty. People of different cultural traditions disagreed. The Irish considered these laws invasions of their right to enjoy legitimate social activities. The Jews, whose day of rest was Saturday, regarded the Sunday laws as a means of forcing them to observe a Christian custom. Both groups wished education to preserve their own heritage rather than to further assimilation, as the reformers expected.

The recurrent crises led occasionally to open violence, more often to intolerant movements. The Know-Nothings in the 1850's and the A.P.A. in the 1890's sought frankly to stir up anti-Catholic sentiment, with limited local success, and the threat remained. After 1900 there was also a significant development of anti-Semitism. And both forms of intolerance reached their apogee in the 1920's and 1930's when the Ku Klux Klan and the Silver Shirts enlisted millions of new members to further their causes.

Ultimately, the restrictive movements failed. By the time the great waves of nineteenth-century immigration swept across the Atlantic, the tradition of religious liberty was strong enough to resist erosion. A congressional committee, considering the Sunday laws in 1830, concluded that the Constitution regarded "the conscience of the Jew as sacred as that of the Christian" and made it the duty of the government "to affirm to *all* — to the Jew or Gentile, Pagans, or Christians — the protection and advantages of our benign institutions."

Moreover, by then liberty had acquired another dimension. The respect for the right of the individual conscience, which at first had focused on relations to God, in time extended also to relations to government and gave birth to a broad, new conception of political liberty. This new concept was intimately connected with the peopling of the country and provided Americans of all backgrounds and faiths with firm safeguards of their freedom.

V

POLITICAL LIBERTY

In 1776, young Thomas Jefferson undertook the most important assignment of his life, that of drafting the text of the resolution by which the Continental Congress dissolved the connection of the American colonies with Britain. In most cases, the phrases flowed easily from his pen: the thoughts they expressed were familiar to him and to his future readers. But when he came to enumerate the grievances against King George III he had to search hard for an appropriate word to express what he wished to say. All along, when he referred to the Americans for whom he spoke, he had used the word "people": one people, rights of the people, people at large; sometimes he had said, "we" or "our." But at one point, he noticed that he had written, "our fellow subjects taken captive on the high seas"; and the word "subjects" seemed incongruous to him. That was hardly the appropriate designation for the people of independent states. Searching his mind for a term that would describe the participants in the political system about to emerge, Jefferson hit upon the word "citizens," which thereafter, first in America and then in Europe, came to describe the relationship of free men to free government.

The word was novel in 1776, but the relationship it described had a long history in the New World. By the time Jefferson wrote, the distinction between citizens and subjects had become one of the features that distinguished Europe from America.

Long before Europeans became aware of America, they were familiar enough with the elaborate instruments through which power governed their actions. The villager and the townsman paid taxes and knew that magistrates would punish infractions of the law.

Immigrants arriving at Castle Garden

Each locality was part of a state ruled by royal authority. From the king power reached downward to control every individual. Questions about the necessity of the order thus imposed arose only during great crises when disputes among the governors upset the pattern.

Most people were subjects, part of a system about which they rarely asked questions. Even the great officeholders, the members of parliaments, and the justices, could act only insofar as the royal mandate instructed them to. The great mass of the population in the Old World was generally passive, its duty clear and simple — to obey.

Liberty therefore meant primarily the absence of restraint. A man was free insofar as no law restrained his actions and no collector took away in taxes or dues what he earned by his labor. Regarded in this negative light, liberty was not uniform; but like all privileges, it was dependent upon status. The freedom of a peasant was not identical with that of a nobleman; each enjoyed the rights commensurate with his wealth, power, and position. Men of all ranks shared a concern with the salvation of their souls; and in the seventeenth century, the claims of conscience led some to disobedience and others to exile when the state intruded. But in most earthly matters power was a subject for conflict among a very small number who shared it. Although occasional utopian thinkers dreamed of a differently organized power structure, their dream was far from reality. For a long time, political considerations influenced but a tiny minority of the population, and few within that minority were in a position to move.

On the surface, little seemed to change in the eighteenth century, in Europe or in America. The political system of the colonies remained within the familiar forms until the American Revolution. The governors were royal officials, the assemblies were little parliaments, and English law was in force. Effective control remained within the hands of a few.

There were, however, significant differences behind the façade. The feudal system did not take hold. There was no aristocracy; and the law did not take account of differences among nobles, burghers, and peasants. All free men were counted alike in rights and privileges. Moreover, as a matter of practice, power slipped into local hands so that even people of relatively humble circumstances found themselves participants in government rather than merely passive subjects. Above all, the colonists slowly but steadily defined a concept of rights that were theirs not by a grant from the king or as a privilege connected with status but simply theirs as human beings.

These differences were a matter of necessity. Only thus was government in the New World effective. New Jersey, hoping to attract newcomers, assured settlers of trial by jury in public proceedings and forbade imprisonment for debt. The fundamental rights were to remain inviolate. The foundation of the government was itself a fundamental law, a statement of rights and privileges that no subsequent statute could alter. "There we lay a foundation for after ages to understand their liberty as men and Christians," West Jersey proclaimed in 1677, "that they may not be brought in bondage, but by their own consent; for we put the power in the people."

In the century that followed, the colonists slowly

and imperfectly, but steadily, worked out the form of their government. They were far from a democracy as later Americans would understand it. But nevertheless they adhered to two cardinal tenets: government ruled by the consent of the governed; and men held certain natural and inalienable rights that no power could override. These ideas were self-evident by the time Jefferson put them into words in the Declaration of Independence. When foreigners, in the eighteenth century, described the liberty of the colonists, this is what they had in mind.

The American Revolution was thus a culmination rather than a beginning. It seemed a grand event in the history of mankind, not only because it cast off the yoke of the mother country but also because it created a new political system, which consolidated the developments of the past and made them permanent for the future. The participants in the Republic were citizens with rights assured against interference by the state. The American thus enjoyed a status that had no counterpart in the Old World.

There was no immediate rush of Europeans, avid to enjoy the blessings of American citizenship. The mass of men was immobile, too depressed even to dare to aspire to the privilege.

A few fixed their eyes on goals unattainable at home but available across the ocean. Tom Paine was such a man. Son of a Quaker corset maker in England whom success always eluded, Paine failed at one occupation after another. He had hardly settled down into marriage when his wife died; a second try ended in divorce. Yet he believed that he had something to say if only he could have freedom to speak. In 1774, at the age of

thirty-seven, he came to Philadelphia, armed with a letter of introduction to Benjamin Franklin. Paine eked out a living with hack work for a year. Then, in January 1776, he published a phenomenally successful pamphlet, *Common Sense,* which sold 120,000 copies in three months because it summed up for Americans the whole meaning of the revolution they were about to launch.

The number of immigrants like Paine grew later in the eighteenth century as a result of the disturbances that followed the disintegration of the old feudal order of Europe. Each upheaval that challenged the existing political system produced refugees. Out of office or in danger of persecution, they found asylum across the Atlantic. Often they were men of education, literate and articulate and capable of making their influence felt far beyond the smallness of their numbers.

The French Revolution in 1789 released a flow that continued for a quarter of a century. The Bourbons had ruled the most stable and the most powerful kingdom in Europe; their fall was a shock in every court of the Continent and the aftereffects spread far beyond the borders of the country in which it occurred. With the collapse of the old regime, the expectation of change spread to Germany, Italy, Ireland, and even England. This revolution, unlike that in England a century and a half earlier, was secular and it aimed at political and social rather than religious change. It was therefore prolonged and spasmodic, following no simple course but rather shifting in unexpected directions as its objectives changed. It took France first from absolutism to limited monarchy, then to a republic, to a directorate, to an empire, and finally to a restoration

Amid the bustle of disembarking immigrants in this detail from an 1855 painting, the wooden trunk at lower right — bearing the crude letters "Pat Murfy for Ameriky" — poignantly symbolizes the hopes of the nearly eight million people who entered "Ameriky" through Castle Garden. The Staffordshire plate at left shows the circular structure — originally a fort, later a concert hall — as it appeared prior to its use as an immigrant processing depot.

These turn-of-the-century photographs graphically illustrate the conditions that immigrants were willing to endure in order to reach America. Crowding every inch of deck space aboard the Atlantic passenger ship at left is an anonymous mass of humanity in which almost all individuality has been lost. Close-up photographs (right and left below) capture family groupings.

of the Bourbons in 1815. Each twist of fortune produced another wave of exiles who sought refuge in the United States.

The first French aristocrats who fled from the reach of revolutionary power went to nearby areas in the Rhineland, from which they confidently expected to return to their previous positions of power. The failure of their efforts to invade France, despite the support of the great powers, and the unfolding terror directed against their families, convinced some that they would be safer in the United States. After them came successive mournful bands of victims of the frequent change of political fortune, as the French Revolution spun its course. The culmination came when Napoleon Bonaparte made himself emperor and thereby antagonized alike the supporters of tradition and the radical republicans. Since he would not tolerate dissent, his opponents often could find safety only in flight. The final irony came with the restoration of the Bourbons, which sent some defeated Bonapartists scuttling to the safety of the United States. In all, well over 10,000 — perhaps as many as 25,000 — Frenchmen crossed the Atlantic during the revolutionary troubles.

Disturbances in Hispaniola added to the migration. The collapse of French power at home weakened the colonial administration and permitted a bloody slave uprising, which succeeded. The white former master class fled, some of them to the nearby republic on the mainland, where they mingled with the growing French community.

America was a refuge to Frenchmen of every political complexion. In the light of their romantic ideas about nature, the New World glistened, in distinct contrast with the discouraging spectacle of European corruption about them. Despotism and superstition seemed to thrive in the Old World whether the Bourbons or the Jacobins held power. No one there was happy, neither rulers nor subjects. Germaine Necker, better known as Madame de Staël, wrote in 1799 that she knew no one who would not at once willingly change his fate with that of a peaceful inhabitant of America. She herself always found a reason to postpone her migration — poor health, a change of lovers, a new marriage. But the bearers of many distinguished names did arrive although not all stayed: Chateaubriand, Talleyrand, Albert de Beaumetz, La Rochefoucauld-Liancourt, Comte de Ribbing, the future King Louis Philippe, and Joseph Bonaparte.

They were indeed a miscellaneous and somewhat incongruous lot — aristocrats behaving like plain citizens in the near wilderness. They clustered in the leading cities, especially in Philadelphia, where the bookshop of Moreau de Saint-Méry was a favored meeting place. Anthelme Brillat-Savarin, the author and gourmet, was happy as a violinist and French teacher in Boston; this happiness, he later wrote, he owed to the fact that he made every effort to behave like an American. Or if the excess of democracy was displeasing, as it was to Chateaubriand, there was at least consolation in nature. Many a wellborn exile made a surprisingly nice adjustment to circumstances in the rural countryside. On an American farm the Marquise Henriette Lucie de La Tour du Pin, once lady-in-waiting to Queen Marie Antoinette, rose before dawn to do the laundry and churn butter. James Donatien Le Ray de Chaumont had actually crossed

This 1885 painting by Andrew Melrose of fashionable couples and relatively prosperous immigrants enjoying an afternoon stroll

recalls an earlier time — when Castle Garden functioned as a reception center for distinguished visitors to New York City.

the Atlantic before the outbreak of the Revolution, but the turmoil in France persuaded him to stay. He built a home in Jefferson County, New York, at a place that came to called Le Raysville and devoted the fifty-five years he spent there to the improvement of local agriculture. Hyde de Neuville, an aristocrat who remained loyal to the Bourbons, nevertheless learned to value the liberty and equality of the New World. Born yesterday, the new nation he decided was not shackled by prejudices or tradition as the old ones were.

The French Revolution had serious international repercussions. Radicals everywhere in Europe believed that the hour of liberation had come, and they prepared to fight for it with sword or at least pen. Alas, they more often knew the taste of defeat than of victory and in the end the only safety for some was flight. Joseph Priestley, the discoverer of oxygen and a distinguished scientist, had his house sacked in 1791 because he had championed the cause of the American colonies and of the revolution in France. Three years later, at the age of sixty-one, he escaped to Pennsylvania where he was free to continue his work. At about the same time, his friend Thomas Cooper also decided that English air was uncongenial to freedom and came to America. Cooper's life continued strenuous; he practiced law in Philadelphia until Jefferson found him a professorship at the University of Virginia. But the perennial rebel could not restrain his advocacy of liberty: he was imprisoned for newspaper attacks on President John Adams, and his unorthodox religious views forced him to leave the University of Virginia and later also South Carolina College, where he became increasingly unpopular by insisting on

delivering an annual lecture denouncing the Bible.

The French Revolution also turned into a prolonged war between France and England and thus encouraged efforts to gain independence for Ireland, which had long been aggrieved by its subjection to Britain. Irish nationalism was strong enough to produce occasional eruptions, but it was not strong enough to lead to victory. It too yielded its quota of refugees. The defeat of the insurrection of the Society of United Irishmen under Lord Edward Fitzgerald in 1798 and the failure of another uprising five years later led to the migration of the leaders who escaped with their lives. Thomas Addis Emmet, son of a doctor in Cork and a fiery orator, was the best-known of these exiles. He arrived in New York City and remained to make a distinguished career as a lawyer and a leader of the Democratic party.

The United States encouraged the immigration of the rebels. Americans believed that it was the destiny of the Republic to serve as a model that would before long be emulated elsewhere. They therefore viewed the battle against monarchism in other countries with sympathy and willingly opened the gates of their country to those who suffered in the common struggle. There was a moment of panic in 1798 when fears of a foreign conspiracy led to the passage of four alien and sedition acts. These laws lengthened the residence requirement for citizenship, gave the president power to expel foreigners during wartime, forbade plots against the government, and punished defamatory criticism of it. But revulsion against these measures was so widespread that the Federalist party, responsible for them, went down to the defeat from which it never recovered;

and the offensive laws were themselves soon repealed. Americans saw themselves as guardians of liberty and could not stomach acts inconsistent with that vision.

The disappearance of the Federalists expressed the general disapproval of a specific policy. But it was also the sign of a profound transformation in American political life. Under the Jeffersonians who took office in 1801 and even more under the Jacksonians a quarter-century later the role of the citizen expanded. In the nineteenth century he was expected not only to consent to be governed but also to participate directly in managing the affairs of the state. The eighteenth-century assumption that the ablest and best-educated would hold office on behalf of the masses crumbled. Increasingly the masses insisted that they were the best custodians of their own rights; and limitations on the suffrage and on the privilege of holding office dropped away. Political liberty thus acquired an added dimension at a time when a new generation of Europeans turned in its search to America.

Although the French Revolution had ended in reaction, it had weakened the old political system and had destroyed many of the small feudal German states. The outcome, however, was not the emergence of a liberal regime in the center of the Continent but rather the steady rise in power of two autocratic empires, Prussia and Austria. In the half-century after 1815, the Hohenzollern and the Habsburg rulers of those countries repeatedly fended off challenges to their power. Although the towns and even more so the universities were centers of dissension, the dissidents lacked the power to make their demands for change effective and often they too departed into exile.

Karl Follen, a revolutionary poet, fled in 1817 to escape the police crackdown on students. In the New World, he found a post as a teacher at Harvard, married into a good family, and became known as a Unitarian minister and abolitionist. His contemporary Francis Lieber had a more difficult time. At first it was all he could do to keep going, with the fees he received for giving swimming and gymnastic lessons in Boston. Then he got an appointment at South Carolina College. *"Mein Gott,"* he exclaimed after some experience with the unruly boys there, "All this for two thousand dollars!" In time he moved on to Columbia University and to a distinguished career as a political economist.

Repressive measures did not permanently stifle German discontent, which burst forth once more in the 1830's. Gustave Koerner, a trained jurist, got into trouble with the authorities after a street fight in Munich. He took part in an unsuccessful uprising in Frankfurt in 1833, then found it prudent to flee to America. He wandered through the West and finally settled in St. Clair County, Illinois, in a community of German farmers. Entering politics, he became a judge; and when he returned to Europe decades later, it was as ambassador of his adopted country to Spain.

Koerner and his contemporaries, having settled down to respectability, became known as the "Grays" when a later group of "Green" revolutionaries arrived from Germany after the failure of the uprising of 1848. The old and the young jostled for places of leadership, and in time, of course, the young won; but by the time they did they had themselves grown old and had themselves settled down.

Carl Schurz was a student at the University of Bonn,

not yet twenty years old, when the excitement started. The imprisonment of a respected teacher Gottfried Kinkel was a challenge. Schurz spent nine months planning to get the old man out of the fortress of Spandau and earned international acclaim when the plot succeeded. For a while Schurz lived in Paris and London, where other revolutionaries also kept alive the hope of reaching power. But in 1852 he concluded that the best chance for a life of liberty lay across the ocean, and he came to America. Westward wanderings brought him to Wisconsin, led him into politics and journalism, and eventually made him famous on both sides of the ocean.

Dr. Carl Munde, wounded in the Dresden insurrection of May 1849, brought a physician's skill to New York. He there introduced the "water cure" and later in western Massachusetts he developed an establishment that offered relief to hundreds. Perhaps out of nostalgia for the Old World, he got the staid Yankees to name the community Florence, after the Italian city he would never see again.

Schurz and Munde moved in company with perhaps three thousand others, mostly people of some education and skill who took their talents to every part of the United States. They were strangers in language and were often critical of the manners and habits of their adopted country. But political liberty offered them the scope to write and speak and argue and vote, and transformed them from revolutionaries to citizens.

The revolutions of 1848 also brought to America an occasional refugee who did not plan to remain permanently but wished rather to use the New World as the base from which to renew the attack upon the European status quo. Of these sojourners, the most colorful was Giuseppe Garibaldi, the same belligerent adventurer who would later cross Bartholdi's path in France.

Garibaldi's life was rich in paradox and in fantasy. This battler for Italian nationalism was a native of Nice, then a part of France; an uncompromising republican, he helped make Italy a monarchy; an idealist, he was forever spoiling for a fight. He spent his early years at sea, then joined the Young Italy revolutionary movement and, in 1834 at the age of twenty-seven, participated in a fiasco of a plot that forced him into exile in South America. He was a pirate for a while, then fought with Uruguay against Argentina, and in 1848 at the smell of trouble returned to Italy looking for action. He found it in Rome, where an uprising had ousted the pope and had led to the formation of a republic, in the defense of which Garibaldi joined. He failed, but failure made him famous; and when he fled in 1849, sympathetic compatriots everywhere were ready to lend a helping hand, which he was not reluctant to grasp. He visited an admirer in Tangiers for six months, then made his leisurely way to New York City, where he was the hero of a little Italian community. Fine! He could live a quiet pleasant life on Staten Island, and even have a nice income from an undemanding job in a friend's candle factory. But boredom quickly set in and with it a desire for action. Garibaldi took to the sea once more and by 1854 was back in Italy sniffing for a hint of battle.

The failures of 1848 made exiles of the leaders of Young Ireland too. John Mitchel and Thomas D'Arcy McGee took refuge in New York when the power of Britain proved too strong to be shaken that year. From

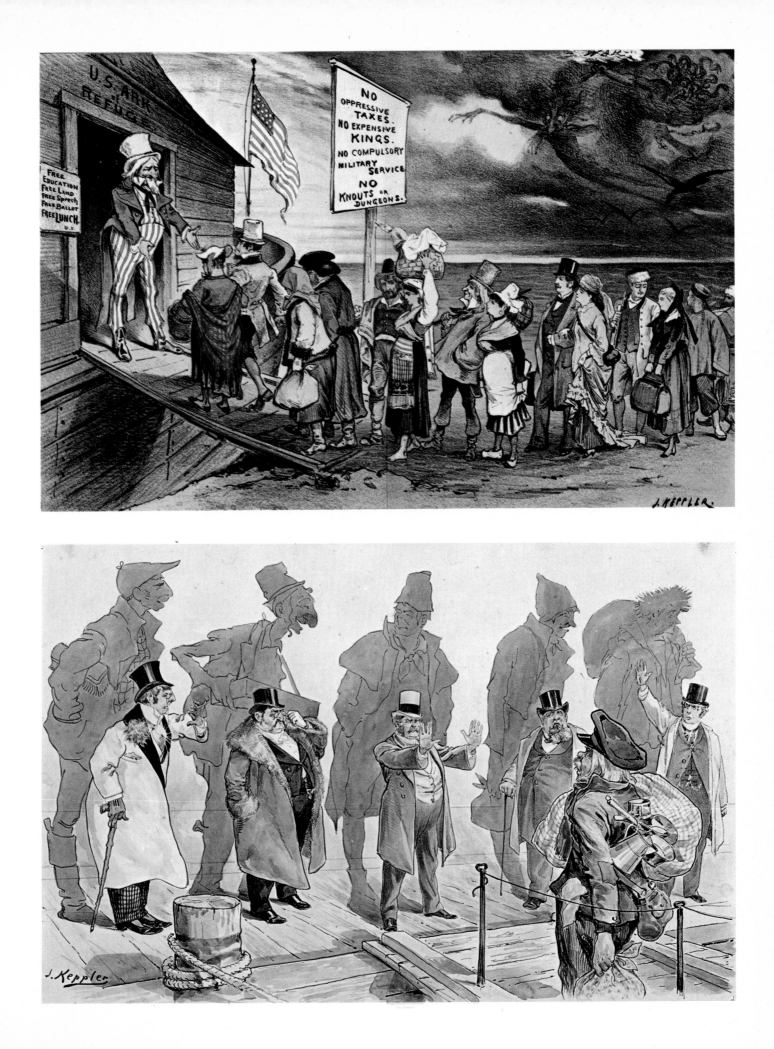

Public outrage over the scandalously inadequate facilities at Castle Garden forced its closing in 1890. By 1906, when this photograph was taken, the former immigration station had been converted into an aquarium and the Battery promenade itself had regained some of its social cachet. Moored to the pier at the far left is the excursion boat that carried afternoon visitors to the nearby Statue of Liberty.

the speaker's platform and the printed page they set to work, in the effort to develop a national consciousness among the swelling population of Irish-Americans. And indeed the hearts of many men and women burned with resentment at the English oppressors of their country, although what to do about it was not clear. Ten years later John O'Mahoney, another young romantic refugee, founded the Fenian movement, which gained steadily in membership, organized a government in exile, printed money, raised an army, and in 1866 launched a futile invasion of Canada in the fanciful notion of thus liberating the homeland. Political liberty for the Fenians as well as for Garibaldi meant simply one thing, the opportunity to prepare for a return to Europe.

The space and political freedom of the New World also offered an opportunity to those who wished neither to go back nor to become citizens but who wished to use American land as a stage on which to conduct radical social experiments without interference. Native Americans had dreams of their own, which they sought to realize in communities like Brook Farm or Fruitlands; and religious sects of diverse origins had long come to America for that purpose. But the nineteenth century witnessed the arrival also of the bearers of secular blueprints for social reform.

The English socialist Robert Owen bought New Harmony, Indiana, from the Rappites in 1825. His plan was clear enough in outline, and he had the aid of his vigorous son Robert Dale Owen as well as of a stormy and contentious Englishwoman Frances Wright. Nevertheless, the project quickly foundered because of internal dissension, and Miss Wright's own Nashoba

Community lasted scarcely longer than had Owen's.

Two decades later Etienne Cabet led five hundred followers from France to Fannin County, Texas, where they planned to put into practice the principle of cooperation described in his romance *Voyage en Icarie*. After the first settlement in 1848, the Icarians established branches in Illinois and elsewhere. But they too suffered the wounds of brotherly quarrels, and within the decade their colonies collapsed. The faith in a just order in which each contributed according to ability and received according to need ran aground again as mortals proved readier to receive than to contribute.

By Bartholdi's time the flow of political refugees from Europe to the United States had subsided. The regimes in power in the Old World had learned to tolerate dissent. After 1870 aggrieved Englishmen, Irishmen, Frenchmen, and Germans could agitate with relatively little interference. Tight restraints survived in Eastern Europe; but rebels from the Balkans and the tsar's domains preferred to find shelter in Switzerland, France, or England, which were close to the scenes of possible action. Besides, the style of life in Europe was more to the taste of people who had no desire to become American citizens but who wished to alter the political system of their native lands.

Nevertheless, American cities still supplied a setting for individual refugees in quest of political liberty. Well into the twentieth century, the fighters for Irish independence or home rule retained bases in New York and Boston. The Clan na Gael, formed in 1867, took up the task of the Fenians and for decades directed the attention of Irish-Americans to the problems of

the homeland. Other organizations carried forward the struggle as particular objectives or tactics shifted from time to time. And it was appropriate that the first president of the Irish republic, when it finally appeared, was Eamon de Valera, born in New York.

The poet José Martí, who had witnessed the popular reception of Bartholdi's statue, knew the meaning of political liberty from his own experience. The Spanish authorities in Cuba had sentenced him, while still a boy in his teens, to labor in the quarries. Then they deported him. After many wanderings, he made New York his base and in the pages of *La patria*, the newspaper he published there, called untiringly for Cuban independence. In 1894 he at last readied an expedition to seize by arms what words had not gained. But it got no farther than Florida, and a second effort a year later, which did reach Cuba, brought him to the skirmish in which he died. In New York a junta of his countrymen carried on the struggle and in time succeeded with American help.

Boston was the nursery of another, and more esoteric, small nation — Albania. A few thousand immigrants from the Adriatic provinces of Turkey worked in the mills of Massachusetts early in the twentieth century — poor, crowded into communal tenements, and utterly strange to the world about them. In 1908 they attracted the attention of Faik Bey Konitza, a well-to-do Harvard student from the same region, who began to publish a newspaper, *Dielli,* for them. His friend Fan Stylian Noli at about the same time founded and became first bishop of an Albanian national church; and the two men together organized a federation of fraternal societies to unite their countrymen. These

activities enabled the Bostonians-by-adoption to play a prominent part in the creation of the new state when the twists of international politics gave Albania independence; and several thousand actually returned from New England for that purpose.

The failure of the Russian revolution of 1905 produced a new wave of emigration. The tsar seemed to consolidate his hold on power during the next decade and the prospects of radical change receded. Some of the exiles then came to the United States. Among them were the aristocratic Aleksandra Kollontai, a pacifist and novelist who later returned to her homeland and to a post in the Soviet diplomatic service, and Leon Trotsky, who left New York after the overthrow of the tsar in February 1917 and reached Russia in time to help stifle the liberal democracy that briefly flickered in the war-torn land.

The revolution in which Trotsky participated altered the relationship of the New World to the Old. After 1917 neither Europe nor America was what it had been in Jefferson's day. Europeans no longer made a simple choice between a feudal old regime and a liberal democracy along the American model. A new more radical revolutionary movement competed for their allegiance. Meanwhile a great scare spread across the United States as Americans became fearful of change and suspicious of the advocates of rebellion.

The events in Russia after 1917 provided lurid illustrations of the dangers of great social upheaval; but concern about the Red menace actually dated back to the 1880's and 1890's. It had been all very well to encourage liberal democrats to rise against their kings; cultivated men like Schurz could move in the best

The Puck *cartoon below was printed October 27, 1886, the day before the statue was unveiled, which may explain the artist's inaccuracies of detail. Liberty stands firm despite the alien forces that threaten to topple her: socialism, anarchism, Georgism (the single-tax movement founded by Henry George), boycott (a sanction employed by discontented laborers), and intolerance. The 1895 drawings at left portray four satiric versions of the statue as it might have looked had it been donated by Germany — a lusty barmaid with a stein of beer and a pretzel; England — Queen Victoria holding sacks of money; China — a coolie with a ballot and a bundle of laundry; and America's millionaires — a tiny statue atop an enormous pedestal, a jibe at their failure to provide funds for its construction.*

circles and were certainly no threat to American institutions. But there was no such assurance about extending the same welcome to anarchists or Communists whose bombings, as at Chicago's Haymarket Square in 1886, were a hazard to everyone. A terrorist had assassinated President McKinley in 1901; and a succession of violent attacks on conspicuous buildings thereafter kept the country on edge. Perhaps it was all part of a conspiracy to subvert the Republic!

Now the immigrants whose numbers still mounted took on a sinister appearance. After only a brief period of residence, they became citizens and then the ballot box put power within their reach. They might not put it to good use. Already the urban political machines were a source of corruption. There would be worse to come unless the United States halted the flow of the alien tide. The mass of foreigners might serve as tools of a sinister international plot against the nation. People troubled by these doubts saw their worst fears confirmed as events unfolded in Russia and in Europe after 1917. Under these conditions, many Americans preferred to withdraw into isolation and to shut their country's gates against future exiles. Changes in the law in 1921 and 1924 ended the tradition of hospitality by narrowly limiting the total admitted annually.

Yet by then the currents of immigration had already generated a force that would revitalize the concept of which Bartholdi's monument was the symbol. For a half-century more the Statue of Liberty would light the way to safety for refugees from a new kind of oppression. And a host of men and women who had escaped want shared the burden of keeping the torch uplifted.

VI

FREEDOM FROM WANT

Wants always constrained men and women. Deprivation chained them. Those without strength lived in
helpless misery. Those with some power struggled for
the liberation that came with relief from the pressure
of want.

The most common wants were the most fundamental. The daily bread that eased the pangs of
hunger; the clothes and shelter to protect the body
against the cold and rain; and the means of providing
for the children's future — these ingredients of survival occupied the thoughts and energies of most
humans in most places at most times. To secure them
people bowed their backs in labor or in prayer. These
needs were the great ends of life for those who knew
that without them they would perish.

The wants of a fortunate minority were more extensive. Those who had bread enough hungered for cake;
possession of a house stirred the appetite for luxurious
furnishings; and the toiler, released from bondage to
the plow, raised his head to glimpse the vision of a
life of ease and enjoyment. New desires grew with the
satisfaction of basic needs so that people no longer
anxious about survival felt a concern almost as intense
for a rise in their status.

Freedom from want was therefore a goal attractive
to all. Few people ever really expected to reach the
earthly paradise in which the satisfaction of desire
would leave them free of care. But however great or
small the hope of success, the mere promise was enough
to justify the struggle for this freedom.

With the discovery of America, Europeans also discovered opportunity. As information about the New
World spread, widening circles caught a glimpse of

A colorfully dressed gypsy at Ellis Island

what freedom from want might mean. At first, a few came to seek it. The multitudes followed.

The earliest arrivals were adventurers accustomed to taking risks and to exploiting opportunities as they turned up.

Merchants sought the opportunity to enrich themselves from the gold, the silver, or the furs reputed to be so abundant in the New World. They learned soon enough that the legends were false; this was not the way to wealth for the majority.

But there were other, and greater, sources for the resourceful, the cunning, and the lucky. A procession of traders moved westward, buying and selling, borrowing and lending, speculating and investing. The attraction that drew them on was usually not gold but opportunity. An expansive society created chances for enterprise. And hostility to privilege or monopoly created and preserved an environment of freedom in which everyone could try his hand at those chances. Andrew Faneuil, for instance, was one of the Huguenots who fled France at the revocation of the Edict of Nantes in 1685. His first resting place was Holland, where he married; but judging the field freer in the New World, he came to Boston and in the 1690's was trading actively with Europe and the West Indies. His nephew and heir, who continued his business, endowed his adopted city with the building that was to house many communal activities, among them the meetings that led to the Revolution.

Opportunity endured while the country filled up and the nation became independent. In 1837 twenty-one-year-old August Belmont arrived in New York from Germany, a representative of the Rothschilds.

In the decades that followed he channeled European funds into the American economy and helped sustain support for the Union during the Civil War. Henry Villard also came from Germany, but without such influential connections. After a brief period as a journalist, he sold railroad bonds, became president of the Northern Pacific, and helped organize General Electric. Faneuil, Belmont, and Villard were representatives of the aggressive entrepreneurs, alert to the possibilities of a growing country and ready to take the risks that paid off.

Opportunity also beckoned younger sons of a less enterprising type — the offspring of families of wealth or good lineage who lacked appropriate prospects at home. It was a good thing to harden such youths by exposure to life in a new country, particularly if there was the prospect of making a fortune there. They did best in circumstances that indulged the taste for adventure. The son of the Earl of Airlie, for instance, made a go of the cattle ranch in Colorado that was a gift of his father. But the hard routine of agriculture was often less to their tastes, as John Sutherland Sinclair discovered when he tried to manage an enormous prairie farm in North Dakota. The poorest results came from efforts directed specifically at education. Thomas Hughes, famous for his novels of English public school life, failed miserably in his attempt to establish a settlement colony in Tennessee, in the town he grandiloquently named Rugby after the well-known ancient institution.

The abundant land and the reputed wealth of the New World continued to attract speculators. The promoters of the Scioto Company in 1790 persuaded one

*Ellis Island in its heyday as an immigrant depot
(above) and the deserted buildings in 1970 (right)*

thousand Frenchmen to start for America; half reached Gallipolis in Ohio, there to find frustration. Other aspirants of quick gains nevertheless continued to arrive. The gold rush of 1848 swept to California adventurers from every country of Europe and some from Asia and Australia as well, so that overnight San Francisco became a cosmopolitan city.

All such people were mobile. Some stayed briefly and then returned to their homelands. Others became permanent residents of the United States. But their role was that of pathfinders.

Those who followed came in much larger numbers, drawn from among the people squeezed by economic changes in the eighteenth and nineteenth centuries. The pressure of new conditions in the system of production drove away from the places of their birth thousands of families for whom migration was the only alternative to the suffering that a loss of status entailed.

Until then the majority of European peasants lived by the traditional methods of agriculture. They sowed and reaped on small holdings while their cattle grazed on extensive communal fields. This mode of cultivation was not efficient; it was incapable of expanding to take advantage of the markets for food that came with the growth of cities or with the rise in industry.

In many parts of Europe, the effort to modernize agriculture, to combine the farms into larger holdings that could be cultivated scientifically by machines, pressed numerous families to the wall. Forced to surrender their plots, they confronted the grim alternatives of departure or of sinking to the level of hired labor.

The change came earliest and was most drastic in England; its visible evidence was a population surplus that grew in the seventeenth and eighteenth centuries out of which came a good part of colonial migration. The surplus nevertheless persisted well into the nineteenth century and sustained an interest in America.

The same forces operated in southern Germany somewhat later than in England. Along the Rhine and in Bavaria and Württemberg, the rise in the price of farms made it difficult for the small holder to retain his grip on the land. In the eighteenth century, these people already furnished the nucleus of a substantial movement. The flow reached its height between 1815 and 1880. In time, the same economic changes compelled many to leave the land in Scandinavia also. Out of Norway, Sweden, and Denmark came men and women who sought to establish farms on the soil of the Middle West to replace those they had lost at home.

The wants of displaced peasants were simple and the means of satisfaction were available in the New World. Land was scarce in Europe, abundant in America. The families for whom there had been no room east of the ocean found space in Illinois and Wisconsin and there tried to rebuild a familiar way of life.

The task was not so simple for the artisans, who suffered everywhere in Europe from the adverse effects of economic change. Factories that operated with machines were far more efficient than the tools of handicraft workers. Those who lost the source of their livelihood and did not wish to fall into the ranks of the proletariat had no choice but to migrate. When cheap factory-made damask cloth poured onto the mar-

ket, the handloom weavers of Dunfermline in Scotland sank into despondent idleness. Andrew Carnegie's father was not alone in the decision to leave his native land for lack of a suitable alternative.

In time, ingenious mechanics and even trained engineers learned to seek out the opportunities of the New World, where habits had not become rigid and where there was room for innovation. John A. Roebling, for instance, was well-educated, a graduate of the Polytechnicum of Berlin, when he came to Pennsylvania to manufacture wire cable. He believed that great bridges need not rest on heavy pillars but could hang from the iron cables he determined to spin. In 1844 the idea worked in the bridge he built across the Allegheny River, and ten years later he threw an astounding span across the Niagara. He was then ready to begin the monumental Brooklyn Bridge, which his son would complete.

Economic change in Europe also ultimately affected trade. As communications improved, the petty dealers who had been intermediaries between the peasants and the rest of the population lost their function. Centralized markets, banks, and distribution systems took customers away from the local brokers who had formerly handled the flow of goods between town and country. The Jews of Eastern Europe thus lost the role they had once played in the economy and, finding few other places open to them, joined the flow of population to the New World.

Opportunity drew the immigrants on — from the marketplaces of Poland and from the rural villages of Scandinavia as well as from the towns of Germany and England. The ability to satisfy want by achievement promised freedom to those who undertook the crossing; willingly they sacrificed present satisfactions for the chance of future gain — of a fortune or a farm or of the means to earn a livelihood with dignity.

America attracted people willing to take the risks of a new start. Here they found everyone mobile, and scarcely anyone contented with his position. Since sons rarely followed the occupations of their fathers, a man's parentage counted less than his skill. In a young nation, full of ambition and just asserting its strength in the world, tradition and precedent mattered less than performance, and new ways were welcome because there was no inherited respect for the old. Foreign travelers were impressed by the vitality of the country; immigrants were challenged to share in it.

There was another aspect to migration, however, the grim features of which Americans then and later preferred not to see. Among the arrivals were millions who came not out of choice but out of need, not through the attractions of opportunity but instead through the pressure of desperation.

Even the tiniest margin of choice was beyond the reach of many Europeans, who were simply passive victims rather than actors in the events around them. At birth their lives fell into grooves from which they could never deviate. Such people passed the years within the limited confines of the village and were totally unprepared when disaster struck and forced them away to the distant strangeness of America.

Among the seventeenth-century immigrants to the colonies there were already substantial numbers of English, Irish, and Scottish servants, sold for a term of years to work in the families of others in return for

The immigrants crowding the ferryboat at far left could admire the Statue of Liberty during their short voyage from the various arrival piers to Ellis Island in upper New York harbor. The 27.5-acre island became the nation's official gateway for new arrivals in 1892, when the federal government assumed responsibility for immigrant processing. The scenes at left of immigrants descending the gangplank and milling about on shore — typical of the frenetic activity at Ellis Island at the turn of the century — contrast sharply with the impression evoked by the photograph below, taken in 1970, of the old ferryboat abandoned and half-submerged in its slip.

their passage. They were not far different from the convicts who were also transported to be sold as servants or, indeed, from the African slaves. Reduced to utter dependence because there was no place for them in the land of their birth, thousands of these British and Irish men wandered the lanes of the countryside until a harsh justice forced them into prison or service — and the difference between the two was not large. The hopelessness of remaining at home was all that eased the fears of the dangers of the journey beyond the ocean.

In the eighteenth century, many German redemptioners came under similar circumstances. Gottlieb Mittelberger described their harsh journey; they suffered through weeks of travel by foot and months at sea, only to reach an alien land where years of arduous labor lay before the promised goal of liberation. Every stage of the transition demanded its victims, who perhaps far outnumbered those who succeeded. Yet the flow continued as long as hope survived — the priceless flicker of a possibility of freedom that did not exist at home.

After Waterloo, the traffic in servants interrupted by a quarter-century of war did not resume. Instead a new and larger migration swept along the most depressed elements of the agricultural population of Europe. Every village contained some cottiers, families without a secure hold on the land, allowed to build the hut in which they lived and to cultivate a tiny plot that provided the food on which they subsisted in return for rent that they paid in labor for others. Decade by decade, their status sank; yet they were immobile for they could not risk the loss of their tenuous place in

the village, which was all they possessed.

When disaster struck, such people were utterly help-less. They had no reserves to carry them beyond a crisis. They perished by the thousands, by the hundreds of thousands.

Between 1846 and 1850 potato rot destroyed the sole means of subsistence of millions of Irish and German peasants. Famine spread. Starvation struck down fam-ilies, villages, counties. The survivors fled. Millions took to the roads, some of whom ultimately wandered to the seaports and on to the New World. Other peoples in other countries repeated the experience later in the century as crop failures produced the same devastating effect in southern Italy, in Greece, in Finland, and elsewhere in Europe and Asia.

Once set in motion, migration came in waves, each larger than its predecessors, until the underlying force was spent. Letters from the early comers encouraged others to follow; eager for comradeship, those already in America reassured hesitant friends. Before long optimistic guidebooks in every language described the good fortune that awaited the wanderers. Ole Ryn-ning's *True Account* (1838) persuaded Norwegians as Morris Birkbeck's *Letters from Illinois* (1818) had the British. Tales, factual or fanciful, by word of mouth or printed page, spread the desire for migration. Far away in Japan in the 1880's, a seventeen-year-old orphan read *The Adventurous Life of Tsurukichi Tanaka,* a Japanese Robinson Crusoe, and straight-away knew that he must come to America. And then, in time, an exile might return home for a visit or to stay. Parading his fortune in an English, Italian, or Greek village, he was a visible inducement to others

Lewis Wickes Hine's eloquent photographs of immigrants at Ellis Island form a gallery of careworn but hopeful faces. At left is his 1905 portrait of a Russian family seated on a bench; below is a modern view of the deserted benches in a waiting room.

The overcrowded facilities at Ellis Island were
host to more than 70 per cent of the 24,000,000
immigrants who entered the country between 1892
and 1954, the year the center was closed. During the
peak year of 1907 as many as 3,000 would-be citizens
were channeled each day through the maze-like
clearance lines (left) in the main building's two-story
registry room. No visas or passports were required
before the 1920's, medical tests were brief, and
personal interviews lasted approximately two
minutes. The yawning emptiness of the depot today
has tempted various groups to propose transforming
the dilapidated buildings into a private college, a
recreational area, an old-age home, a veterans'
convalescent center, a waterfront park — and, most
recently, a rehabilitation center for narcotics addicts.
In 1965 the island was declared a historic shrine and
was added to the Statue of Liberty National
Memorial in recognition of its role as the nation's
foremost immigration gateway.

to go do likewise. Lee Chew was a poor Cantonese peasant of sixteen when a neighbor returned from a city called Mott Street to build a great house that awed the whole district. Lee thereupon determined also to go to the country of wizards and gain some of their wealth.

The desperate eagerness to believe in the New World's wonders deepened among the groups that suffered most from economic change. America alone promised them an escape from hopelessness. The desire to move became a fever. "Furnish me with ships, or free passages, and I could take a quarter of the working population of this country to the United States next spring," wrote an American consul in Sweden in 1863; and his experience was typical.

Freedom from want, to most such immigrants, had a narrow scope. These were not heroic adventurers or seekers after great fortunes but rather fugitives from famine and impoverishment. Rarely did they possess a clearly defined destination. They went where the ships took them and, after landing in the crowded seaports of the Atlantic coast, generally remained where they were. The abundant acres of the West were out of reach of those without the means to get established. Lacking skill or capital, they could not choose their own employment. They took what jobs they could get at whatever wages the bosses were willing to concede. The incomes of laborers were low and costs high in mushrooming new cities that offered little space to strangers. Whoever found work took it, women and children as well as men. Every penny counted, for the day's pay slipped speedily through the fingers of people not accustomed to the ways of buying and sell-

ing, of renting and managing in the urban setting.

Hardship was therefore familiar to those neighborhoods in which most newcomers congregated. Unemployment left many a family in need, and few ever accumulated the resources to cope with the great crises of industrial accidents, prolonged illness, or disease. Crowded into the dense quarters that others abandoned to their use, penned up in wretched housing, and driven by the remorseless quest for daily bread, the immigrant laborers were easy victims of the maladies of the slums — crime, intemperance, and pervasive poverty.

It was no consolation to them that their presence stimulated the American economy. The new arrivals kept replenishing a pool of surplus labor that was available to construct the railroads, build the cities, and man the new and growing factories. They built an industrial system that was the wonder of the world by 1900 but that offered them no immediate reward. They paid the price in suffering. But they were people accustomed to suffering.

Yet harsh as were the conditions they found, the immigrants continued to come, and from ever widening circles. By the end of the nineteenth century factory workers from England, Germany, and Central Europe joined the peasants; the subsidiary streams from China and Japan, from Canada and Mexico, added to the flow from Europe. However difficult the life of labor was in the United States, it continued to attract new settlers.

Fed from all these sources, the total number of aliens admitted to the United States grew astronomically; in the peak decade, 1901–10, fully 8,795,386

entered the country. To people with no other hope America offered the prospect of freedom from want. Great achievements were within the reach of a few, especially those who were young, energetic, and enterprising. Andrew Carnegie's reward was wealth. Others made their marks by invention, public service, or intellect. The sixteen-year-old Serbian Michael Pupin, who landed in 1874 with hardly a dollar in his pocket, worked for months at poorly paid odd jobs, but he reached for an education and became the distinguished scientist whose discoveries made the long distance telephone possible. In 1880, six years after Pupin's arrival, a Hungarian boy of six came off the ship with his parents. The public schools of New York enabled him to gratify the wish to be a doctor. Joseph Goldberger's ambitions were not for a rich practice, however; instead he entered the United States Public Health Service and, working in the South, discovered that pellagra, the scourge of the region, had its source in improper nutrition and its cure in changes in diet. There were enough instances of success, on one level or another, to demonstrate that the dream of freedom from want was not altogether vain.

The losers far outnumbered the winners, however. For many migration was a personal disaster, made tolerable only by the glimmer of a possibility of improvement; and those who could not even clutch at that hope could at least strive to put it within reach of their children. They came with modest expectations, not in the hope of finding fields of gold or of rising to the possession of great fortunes. Knowing that hard work lay before them, they sought not certainty or ease, not even security, but a fighting chance

to earn the freedom from want that was out of their reach in the Old World.

Uncertainty about the ability to absorb the vast armies of the poor who migrated because of want troubled many Americans in the twentieth century. Until then, space had been abundant for the seekers of liberty for every variety of religious faith or political program. But the same freedoms, extended to landless, unskilled laborers might well be hazardous to the Republic. Unfamiliar churches, all equal, might cloak un-American conspiracies; and the instruments of politics, fallen into hands incapable of wielding them properly, might become tools of corruption or even of subversion of the whole social order. Such fears for the future lay behind the movement to restrict immigration that conquered opinion in the 1920's and reduced admissions to a trickle. Only 4,112,000 newcomers entered the United States in that decade, and only 528,000 came in the 1930's. And the demand for manpower during and after World War II was satisfied from within the Western Hemisphere by wetbacks who came illegally from across the Mexican border and by Puerto Ricans who held American citizenship.

The fears were justified. The brutal condition of immigrant life was a cause for concern. But the diagnosis of the disorder and the remedy proposed were alike incorrect. Americans who blamed the problem on some inherent defect in the newcomers' characters expected to correct the ills of the times by closing the gates to further applicants. The cure proved ineffective, because poverty, crime, and other forms of delinquency resulted not from the qualities of one ethnic group or another but from the situation in which the

The need for a Hebrew eye chart in a medical examining room at Ellis Island (left) testifies to the difficulties immigration officials faced in processing the many Europeans who did not speak English. The modern photographs at right of rusting laundry machinery and jumbled stacks of mildewed bed linen recall the crude facilities offered those immigrants who did not pass the superficial examinations and were temporarily detained on the island.

economic and social system placed them all.

Obsession with the misread symptoms blinded many observers to the more significant developments growing out of the experience of the masses who aspired to freedom from want. The immigrants and the native Americans who understood their plight gradually learned that the opportunities and rewards of the New World lay not in mines that yielded fortunes to a few but in the freedom to earn the bread of life in dignity. The men who waited at the factory gates or shaped up for the construction gangs were willing to expend their full energies in competition for the best places and they had a realistic sense of how tough the odds against them were. But they wanted an equal break, a fair chance so that their effort would have meaning and so that they would not be playing in a game with the cards stacked against them.

These people were not social philosophers or political theorists and they lacked the tricks of intellect to help them develop elaborate formal systems. They blundered from one expedient to another, sometimes fumbling into error, sometimes settling for half-a-loaf solutions, often contradicting themselves. Yet in time they — immigrants and natives, laborers and their sympathizers — struggled toward a definition of liberty broader than they had inherited.

Self-help and cooperation — these qualities were central to the change in attitude. Strangers in an alien place knew they could look to no one for help but themselves. No one had asked them to come. No one was responsible for their welfare. No one cared whether they stayed or left, succeeded or failed, perished or survived. In need they could turn only to one another;

and those who had little to spare understood the value of having a helping hand to give.

The villagers of an older world had always worked together, sharing possession of pastures, forests, and streams, executing some tasks each family for itself, others jointly by common effort. And while some were poor and others rich, with interests that differed accordingly, the common fate that identified each with the community silently, inexorably persuaded all to cooperate.

The problem was to adapt these impulses toward self-help and cooperation to the practical terms of life in industrial America. Samuel Gompers tried one way. In 1886 he was thirty-six years old, a veteran of the workshop for he had rolled his first cigars as a boy of ten, well before his family migrated from England to America. It was a nasty, ill-paying job without prospects either in London or in New York; and Gompers, who married at the age of seventeen and thereby assumed a breadwinner's burdens, beat his brains out in the search for an escape. He could sometimes stir his fellows by reading to them from the works of Marx and Engels, but socialism added nothing to the pay packet. On the other hand, organizations like the Odd Fellows, the Foresters, and the Cigarmakers' Union, of which he was a member, gave participants a sense of fraternity as well as practical aid in moments of need. Now he helped form the American Federation of Labor to link local unions into a national association.

His efforts yielded limited gains. Forty-five years later, the A.F. of L. had organized only a small minority of American laborers, mostly skilled craftsmen; the employees in the great mass industries and the

The jaunty man at left may have been one of the many immigrants who received a new name at Ellis Island because an inspector misunderstood his foreign pronunciation. Below, stacks of upended desks and old mattresses flank a deserted corridor.

Although immigrant processing was of necessity impersonal, certain amenities were provided. A uniformed waiter serves a group of Germans in the Hine photograph below. A sign propped against a partition in the deserted dining room (right) once cautioned immigrants — in English, German, Italian, Polish, and Spanish — to conserve food. The mute piano at far right, in sad disrepair, is a reminder that newcomers were occasionally able to find time for amusement during their stay on the island.

unskilled had no protection and had advanced little after decades of struggle. Nevertheless, a start had been made: unions had achieved a recognized place in the industrial system. The garment workers, the miners, and the teamsters, among others, drew strength from the ethnic as well as from the economic loyalties of their members. And a generation of leaders who succeeded Gompers had acquired the experience that enabled them to undertake the greater task of organization awaiting them in the 1930's.

In the interim, palliatives were important. The municipal governments provided facilities for care of the ill, the poor, and the dependent, in some cities supplemented by private voluntary institutions. While the foreign-born usually had no choice in the matter, they hesitated to accept aid given under strange auspices and tried to provide for their own needs. Each of the immigrant churches transplanted a tradition of charity and some groups also supported secular efforts at philanthropy. By the twentieth century, a heterogeneous array of hospitals, orphanages, and various other asylums were evidence of the determination of newcomers to provide their own refuge for the victims of disaster.

Where the need was less immediate and less visible, the response was less clear. The strangers and their children who did not suffer from physical maladies were less easy to serve. They needed not medicine but guidance in the ways of city life. To adjust to the environment and to improve their status they had to know what goals were worth working for and what opportunities were open to them. The desire to provide help of this sort moved Jane Addams to establish Hull House in Chicago in 1889. She was then approaching her thirtieth birthday. Born in Illinois, reared in a prosperous family and well educated, she was still looking for a vocation. Hull House gave it to her. Modeled on settlement houses in England and influenced by the services that the Y's performed for natives, it aimed to draw the city's social classes together by bringing educated and prosperous youth to the slums to share the life of the poor. For Jane Addams and for hundreds like her in scores of cities, this work was an ethical equivalent of religion. And for the people among whom they worked, it opened windows on a wider world than they knew before.

For some, exposure was a call to conscience. Jacob A. Riis, who came as a boy from Denmark, led a life of hard labor until he found a post as a reporter. His work took him among the residences of the poor and in 1890, a year after the opening of Hull House, he published *How the Other Half Lives.* The book did not supply the answer, but it opened the eyes of millions to the problem and it sensitized their consciousness of the challenge of need.

Self-help, cooperation, and even the concern of solicitous outsiders took Americans only part of the way toward freedom from want. Yet few were willing to concede that the goal was unattainable, and the determination to reach it gradually turned the thoughts of many to the possible use of politics as an instrument of improvement. The ballot put the power to govern within reach of the citizens; they had only to apply it properly for their own welfare.

Such ideas made sense to John Peter Altgeld, for one. This man had known hardship firsthand. Brought as an infant from Germany, he toiled on the Ohio farm of his brutal father until he was twenty-one years old. Then, in 1869, Altgeld escaped, but for years he found nothing better to do than drift about as a common laborer. Even after he had studied law, practiced it, and made fortunate investments in real estate, he retained a vivid awareness of poverty. Entering politics, he became governor of Illinois and earned the hostility of many respectable people by pardoning the anarchists convicted after the Haymarket Square riot and by denouncing the use of the federal army against strikers. Nevertheless, his persistent advocacy of reform measures showed the immigrant laborers that politics might be a means of ameliorating their condition.

A generation later, a native of New York City of Irish ancestry moved in the same direction. Alfred E. Smith had come up through the ranks of Tammany Hall, but he was more than a hack politician. He knew the problems of the poor among whom he lived. When the terrible Triangle fire of 1911 took the lives of 143 working girls and dramatized the need for reform, Smith took action. As a legislator and governor, he pushed laws to regulate the conditions of labor, to compensate injured workers, to increase the supply of housing, and to support programs of public health and education.

A president from an old American family completed the transition to government responsibility. Franklin Delano Roosevelt had not had Smith's direct exposure to the life of the poor and he had given little thought to their problems before he entered the White House. But the Great Depression of the 1930's was an effective teacher and swiftly showed how vulnerable all Amer-icans were. The New Deal not only introduced social security and unemployment insurance, not only recognized the legitimacy of collective bargaining and thus permitted the unionization of mass industry, it also acknowledged the obligation of government to further the welfare of the whole population. It gave a fundamental turn to policy by adopting freedom from want as a basic social goal. It thus opened the way for future explorations of the meaning of fairness in employment and of community organization.

The New Deal directed the attention of Americans to internal problems. Out of their contact with immigrants, Americans had extended the concept of liberty, from the first struggles with conscience and from political rights to satisfaction of the basic wants of the whole people. With regard to the outside world, however, the dominant attitude had become one of neutrality and isolation. Few realized that foreign affairs would soon impinge once more upon their fate. Only a trickle of refugees from totalitarian rule abroad reminded the citizens of the Republic that they could not completely cut themselves off from the outer world.

Symbolic of the anonymous millions who passed through Ellis Island, a group of immigrants waits patiently for the ferry that will take them to New York, whose jagged skyline looms in the distance as both a challenge and a promise.

VII

FLIGHT FROM TYRANNY

After 1918, new political forms, which sprouted amidst the wreckage of war in Europe, threatened all aspects of human liberty everywhere. Communism and fascism were not reactionary reversions to earlier types of control. They were types of political organization novel in structure and in aims; and as they spread, they set in motion a new kind of migration, which turned toward the United States as had earlier movements.

The postwar regimes of Central Europe were the products of violence and revolution; they seized power with scarcely a pretext of concern for legality. Claiming to act on behalf of the whole people, they demanded the total integration of society and the total loyalty of individuals. One party controlled all state offices; and every church, industry, association, and medium of expression was coordinated with its will. The leaders who ruled in the name of the masses secured complete obedience by terror or by the threat of terror. Those who refused to conform were in genuine danger of extermination; a fortunate few were allowed to escape.

The first successful seizure of power occurred in Russia. Discontent with the war and the economic misery of the population toppled the tsar in the spring of 1917. A democratic republic then struggled for stability while the old order crumbled away; but the liberal provisional government was scarcely six months old when ruthless revolutionaries, pretending to act on behalf of the workers and peasants, grasped control. In the three years of turbulence that followed the Communists extended their hold over the whole Russian Empire and thereafter maintained it by relentlessly suppressing all potential opponents.

An Italian family arrives at Ellis Island

The decisive nature of the Russian Revolution was quickly apparent to the aristocracy and to the men of great wealth who were its first victims. They took flight earliest. Many of them sought refuge in the capitals of Western Europe, cities that were more congenial to their tastes than were those of the United States. But those with industrial, professional, or intellectual skills crossed the Atlantic where they found the opportunity for a new start.

As the consequences of revolution unfolded, liberals and socialists who would not accept the repressive regime joined the exodus from Russia or attempted to do so. But departure became increasingly difficult after 1924. Few Russians, thereafter, had the funds to get away, and the Soviet authorities closed the country's exits. The possibility of admission to the United States was narrowed by a rigid quota and visa system. The number of fugitives from Communism who reached the United States before 1941 was therefore small, but among them were figures of genuine distinction who made valuable contributions to the life of their adopted country.

Some aspects of American industry gained substantially because of the migration. Before 1914, Russia had been among the world's leaders in aviation; and some of its most talented engineers found the environment across the Atlantic more congenial than that in their native land under the Reds. Igor I. Sikorsky, for instance, was not yet thirty when he fled Russia in 1919, but he was already famous. A graduate of the naval college at St. Petersburg, he had begun to build flying machines in 1908 when he was just about twenty; and in 1913 he had constructed the world's first multi-

motored aircraft. In America he founded a company of his own and designed the helicopter and also the clippers that opened the Atlantic to passenger travel. When he arrived in the United States in 1918, twenty-four-year-old Alexander de Seversky was to be a Russian military attaché in Washington, having by then survived an exciting career as a naval pilot. Instead, Seversky decided to remain in America, set up an aircraft factory that became part of Republic Aviation, and helped significantly in developing the industry.

The contributions of many Russian exiles to scholarship and the arts were fully as important. In the 1920's and 1930's, American universities were just approaching maturity. The undergraduate colleges, football stadia, and fraternities still drew more popular attention than libraries or laboratories. Now the efforts to develop great seats of learning in the universities profited from the remarkable infusion of academic talent from Russia, where the Soviets were stifling the spirit of free inquiry. The sociologist Pitirim A. Sorokin, the historian of the ancient world Michael I. Rostovtzeff, and the expert on Byzantium A. A. Vasiliev were among those eminent Russians who enriched American universities after 1918.

How important was it to acquire the world's leading authority on a given subject? Or just another expert in some academic field?

Sometimes the answer was not apparent on the face of it. Later, in the 1950's, a foreign visitor came to Cambridge, Massachusetts, to see Michael Karpovich, an elderly professor at Harvard, who lived in an old house, overwhelmed by domestic cares and administrative duties. There seemed a kind of sadness within him

to which he gave vent by playing old Viennese waltzes on a broken down piano; life had passed him by and the great books he hoped to leave behind him remained unwritten. So it seemed to his guest.

Yet his life had been a success. When he arrived in 1917 to join the embassy staff in Washington, scarcely an institution in the United States was prepared to teach the Russian language, Russian history, or Russian culture. In the next three decades Karpovich trained a whole generation of scholars in these subjects and thereby helped his adopted country meet the difficulties of international relations it faced after 1941.

The involvement of Russian emigrés in the arts was more visible. The development of the ballet was almost all due to them; George Balanchine, Michel Fokine, and Léonide Massine transplanted the methods and traditions of St. Petersburg to New York. Serge Koussevitsky, who took over direction of the Boston Symphony Orchestra in 1924, was the best known of the musicians who permanently made their homes in the United States. The painter Nicholas L. Vasiliev made the same decision. And Vladimir V. Nabokov, after some years of residence in Europe, finally made his way across the Atlantic. In America he acquired, and in his novels he demonstrated, an eloquent command of the English language.

Italy like Russia suffered grievously during World War I, and it too felt the pressure of ideological groups that struggled for the power to recast society. In Italy, however, such basic institutions as the monarchy and the church had survived intact. Revolution there was accomplished through an agreement between the crown and a socialist adventurer, Benito Mussolini, supreme

American photographer Lewis W. Hine's celebrated studies of Ellis Island faces mirror a wide range of human emotions. Among his subjects (left to right): a stolid Finnish stowaway, a cocksure Russian steel worker, a toothless Czech matriarch, a worldweary Armenian Jew, and a timorous Russian Jewish woman. A less solemn study by an unknown photographer shows a gypsy family (below) arriving at Ellis Island.

leader and prophet of the Fascist movement. Fascism had much in common with Communism. It too claimed trusteeship of the rights of the people; it too aimed to develop a corporate system of society; it too demanded total obedience and was willing to use force without the scruples of conventional legality. But the Fascists were readier than the Communists to encourage collaboration and to make friends of potential enemies, while holding force in reserve for use when needed. The regime gained strength through the 1920's and 1930's; it took World War II to produce its collapse.

Fascism drove into exile men and women of conscience who were unwilling to accept life under the new system. The Italians most likely to leave were intellectuals or scholars who shied away from the accommodations and special arrangements Mussolini was often willing to make to buy off opposition.

Gaetano Salvemini had been a distinguished historian, a man of affairs, and a member of the Italian parliament. When he had been young, a great earthquake had swept away his wife and children and left him the sole survivor of a large family. Perhaps the disaster, having deprived him of everything he valued, had also stripped him of all illusions; but it left him one possession, dignity. He had not hesitated to criticize the government before Mussolini took office, and he was not reticent thereafter. Salvemini considered Fascism absolutely intolerable. The eloquence and vigor with which he said so made it prudent for him to leave Italy. After 1930, he made a new career of teaching and writing in America. G. A. Borghese and a few others joined him in due course. The mass of the Italian population, mainly peasants and workers, however, lacked the means to escape to the United States.

Totalitarianism took its extreme form and had the largest consequences for migration in Germany. The Nationalist Socialist Party, under the leadership of Adolf Hitler, assumed power in 1933 and held it until defeat in a catastrophic war more than a decade later. The Nazis used total force and dealt mercilessly with all opponents. They demanded absolute loyalty and complete control of all social institutions, justifying every means by invoking the national will, on behalf of which they acted. To these features, already familiar in Russia and Italy, the National Socialists added a novel element that increased both their strength and their ruthlessness. They identified themselves as Aryans, guardians of the purity of a bloodstream that had run undefiled through history. Defense of their racial supremacy justified any measures against the lesser subhuman breeds who were doomed to give way to provide living space for the Third Reich and its people. Commitment to this racist ideology imparted a ruthless quality to Nazism that strengthened its resolve to harry dissenters out of the land.

Furthermore, Hitler took power in an advanced industrial society, where government was relatively incorruptible and efficient. Here was none of the sloppiness that left occasional possibilities for evasion in the pattern of terror that had developed in Russia and Italy The German apparatus had all the advantages of scientific expertise and trained personnel. Only those who were permitted to depart for reasons of state escaped.

A selective factor, therefore, operated in the course of the movement of population out of Germany. In general, the Hitler regime allowed only those with sub-

The statue may have symbolized the American dream, but it was often Manhattan that either fulfilled or denied it. Over the decades the great metropolis acted as a vast magnet, drawing Europe's huddled masses to its teeming ghettos. A modern aerial photograph shows both the serene and isolated statue and the mist-shrouded spires of lower Manhattan. The city-wide optimism and vigor that so appealed to turn-of-the-century immigrants is exemplified today by the rising twin towers of the World Trade Center, visible at the upper left.

stantial means to leave. Few workers or peasants could afford the payments that were the price of permission to depart. Those who escaped were almost all middle-class people — doctors, lawyers, professors, teachers and intellectuals, as well as some businessmen.

Perhaps half the refugees were Jews. In 1933, some 600,000 adherents of that faith lived in Germany as they had for centuries. Hitler's racist doctrine identified them as non-Aryan and along with them Christians who had even one Jewish grandparent. Discriminatory measures of mounting severity excluded Jews from the economic and cultural life of the nation and left them the meager choice between departure and a steady decline in status. The intellectual critics of the regime, however pure their ancestry, also found flight prudent.

The contagion spread insidiously to Germany's neighbors. In 1938 Austria became part of the Third Reich and a year later, Czechoslovakia. The Nazi rule spread to both countries with harsh consequences for Jews and dissenters. Fascist Italy, drawn into Hitler's awkward diplomatic embrace, felt obliged to adopt anti-Semitism as an official policy and to tighten further already severe restraints upon personal liberty. And the intervention of Germans and Italians in the Spanish Civil War, while the democracies remained neutral, was a considerable factor in the victory of Francisco Franco's dictatorship. These dismaying events added to the number of fugitives by creating conditions intolerable to men of good conscience.

Flight at first took the refugees to nearby sanctuaries. Europeans preferred a minimal break with the past, costs were lower if there was no long ocean crossing, and a stubborn hope persisted that a turn of events might soon make a return to their native lands possible. But the short steps did not lead to safety. The Germans who fled in 1933 to Austria and Italy witnessed the shadow of the swastika fall across those countries also, and in 1938 they had to take to the road again to France or England. But nowhere in Europe was entry easy; stern immigration authorities manned the barriers at every border and excruciating difficulties stood in the way of securing visas.

Nor was entry to the United States easy. American immigration laws admitted only a small number of newcomers annually and those had to supply stringent guarantees of good character and ability to support themselves. The quota for natives of Germany was large by comparison with that allowed to less fortunate countries, but at that it amounted to fewer than 26,000 a year. Many eager applicants for admission to the United States were therefore disappointed.

Now, as in the nineteenth century, the United States was the best of available destinations in the eyes of the refugees. About 300,000 of them secured admission by the time the war curtailed transatlantic travel. About half of these were Germans and Austrians; the remainder, Poles, Czechs, Russians, Italians, and Hungarians. Some two-thirds were Jews and the great majority were middle-class or in the professions. They arrived in the midst of a depression and faced serious problems of resettlement. It was hard under the best of circumstances for highly trained men to transfer their skills from one society to another, and the tension of the decade magnified the difficulties. Americans, resentful of reminders about international dilemmas from which they wished to be isolated, were then suspicious of foreign-

The bewildered and bereft men and women who passed through the Ellis Island processing pens during the late 1800's were immediately confronted by the harsh disparity between expectation and actuality. New York's Lower East Side was no alabaster city, and Orchard Street (left) was hardly a fruited plain. Rising above their initial disillusionment, the denizens of Manhattan's most famous immigrant area transformed the streets of their ghetto into a vast, colorful, and convivial open-air market where goods were hawked in a dozen languages simultaneously.

ers and particularly of Jews. Times were hard for everyone; there was no disposition, in the 1930's, to ease the way for strangers.

The arts were most receptive, for Americans had long been dependent upon Europe for talent in these fields and no amount of prejudice could obscure the fact that some people had the necessary skills and talents and others did not. The effects in music were particularly striking. Now famous performers and composers came not for the tours of a season but to make permanent homes in the New World. Well over a thousand musicians thus enriched American concert halls, among them such conductors of distinction as Bruno Walter and Otto Klemperer and such composers as Paul Hindemith.

Three architects among the arrivals from Germany were paradoxically able to effect a transformation in building styles toward which native Americans had labored without success for almost a half century. Long before 1930, Louis Sullivan and Frank Lloyd Wright had called upon architecture to come to terms with the machine and to recognize the needs of the technological world. But the dominant modes remained eclectic imitations of past forms, ill-adapted to the times. The prophetic exhortations of Sullivan and Wright gained effective force with the arrival in the United States of Walter Gropius, Marcel Breuer, and Ludwig Mies van der Rohe, all exiles from Germany. Gropius had been director and aesthetic spokesman of the Bauhaus in Dessau, around which had clustered a group of creative architects, designers, and painters who worked toward humane forms adapted to the available materials and the new social environment. As a teacher and

127

practitioner, Gropius exerted tremendous influence on the generation that matured in the United States after 1937 and left a permanent imprint on the American urban landscape. Breuer and Mies van der Rohe were only slightly less important.

By contrast, writers were at loose ends. Of course, a distinguished novelist of Thomas Mann's stature could continue his work without concern and without perceptible influence from the altered surroundings about him. Among the other well-known authors who fled to the United States were Franz Werfel and Lion Feuchtwanger. But some did not recover from the shock of being wrenched from the familiar setting within which they had been creative. Stefan Zweig, for instance, never found a home after the Nazis drove him out of Salzburg. The writer tried life in England, the United States, and Brazil; despondent, Zweig at last resorted to suicide.

The refugees of the 1930's strengthened the American universities even more than had their predecessors of the 1920's. Positions were far from abundant, for the institutions of higher learning were contracting under the pressure of poverty. Often enough, as a result, a world-famous scholar found himself teaching undergraduates in a remote little college without acceptable libraries or laboratories. And academic communities before 1941 were by no means free of prejudice or totally open to talent.

Despite the difficulties, the emigrés exerted an invigorating influence on university life. Later developments focused attention on the work of the physicists. These scientists adapted easily because they had formed an international community for many decades; politi-cal boundaries were not very relevant to their problems and researchers in every part of the world freely exchanged information and ideas to their mutual advantage.

Nazism poisoned the atmosphere in which the physicists worked and they began to leave Europe almost at once. Albert Einstein who had already gained worldwide fame arrived in the United States in 1933; in his wake came the Hungarians Edward Teller and Leo Szilard, the Russian George Gamow, the Swiss Felix Bloch, the German Hans Bethe, the Austrian Victor Weisskopf, and the Italian Enrico Fermi. The efforts of these foreign-born scientists meshed with those of native Americans like Harold C. Urey and J. Robert Oppenheimer, and access to the nation's technology enabled them to complete the dramatic achievement of the atomic bomb. But in the longer perspective, the more consequential outcome was their discovery of the whole new world of nuclear physics.

In numerous other fields, the newcomers had the same stimulating effect on scholarship in the United States. The historians Ernst H. Kantorowicz, Hans Rosenberg, Felix Gilbert, and Hajo Holborn, the sociologists Paul Lazarsfeld, and Theodor W. Adorno, the psychologist Kurt Lewin, the classicist Werner W. Jaeger, and the critic Erwin J. Panofsky were among those who transformed the study of the social sciences and of the humanities.

The practice of the professions was more difficult. Only the psychoanalysts did well, for their numbers were scarce and an unsatisfied demand for their services already existed at the time of their arrival. In the early 1930's, there were psychoanalytical institutes only in

Hine followed his Ellis Island pilgrims on their progress uptown, and there his camera recorded both the exploitation of child labor (left) and the excessive physical burdens borne by immigrant women (right).

New York, Boston, and Washington, and there was no substantial body of trained American analysts. A ready welcome therefore awaited Franz Alexander, Karen Horney, Theodor Reik, Otto Rank, Felix Deutsch, and Erich Fromm, all of whom were already well-known by reputation and who made their adjustment to the New World with ease.

On the other hand, lawyers trained in Europe were rarely able to adapt their learning to the requirements of the bar in the United States and generally had to retool for some other occupation. Physicians and dentists also had a hard time of it, not because their medical training was deficient but because restrictive licensing laws prevented them from exercising their skills effectively. Nor could businessmen readily transfer their activities to the United States in view of the hard times that affected all enterprise during the 1930's.

Nevertheless the migration went surprisingly well. A number of philanthropic and religious agencies eased the process of adjustment; and the refugees themselves were quick to help one another once they passed through the first stages of resettlement. Little associations and cultural organizations sprouted wherever there were large concentrations of immigrants; *Aufbau,* a German-language newspaper published in New York City, provided them with an organ of communication. The children of these newcomers moved readily into every aspect of the life of their adopted country.

Before the decade was over, a new international catastrophe caused a massive displacement of population that far overshadowed the problems of the emigrés of the 1930's. A second and greater world war threw Europe into turmoil, and the march of armies across the Continent drove millions of persons out of the rubble of their homes. In the years when German power expanded, the ferocious policy of the Nazis incarcerated hundreds of thousands of helpless civilians in great concentration camps and transferred others in untold numbers to forced labor away from their native lands. When peace finally returned to a ravaged Europe, perhaps 40,000,000 displaced persons were stranded in miserable dependency, far from their places of origin, with no destination to which they could readily return. To complicate matters, changes in boundaries and new revolutions altered the map of Europe so that many lacked even the hope of ever getting back to a familiar setting.

The major task of resolving the problem of these people fell upon the European countries. Germany absorbed large numbers of them and many East Europeans returned, though unwillingly, to their birthplaces. But political, religious, and economic obstacles prevented others from going back. Many of them dreamed wistfully of escape to the United States.

American immigration policy, however, stood in the way. During the war and in the crisis immediately thereafter cumbersome administrative arrangements as well as the old law restricted admissions; every applicant needed a visa and an individual sponsor within the United States. Therefore only a meaningless fraction of the immense total that needed a place of refuge got in — 16,836 in 1947, for example.

A campaign to bring immigration policy abreast of the new conditions bore a minor measure of success when the acts of 1948 and 1950 permitted the admission of about 400,000 displaced persons by the end of

1952. Narrow points of entry also existed for other exceptional individuals so that perhaps 2,000,000 newcomers in all arrived in the ten years after the war.

As the active fighting subsided, many people in all parts of the world discovered that they had moved into a period not of peace but of intermittent conflict darkened by the frightening pall of atomic weapons, which held the power to destroy all civilizations. After Hiroshima, and even more so after more than one power possessed the bomb, no one in office could forget that the rashness of a statesman or the miscalculation of a soldier might blow up in an instant what men had labored for thousands of years to create. Caution under these circumstances was the only sane policy.

Yet there remained profound sources of instability. The war itself had left numerous boundaries imprecise — in Central Europe, in Korea, and in Southeast Asia. The United Nations Organization, upon which many hopes at first fastened, proved incapable of resolving conflicts or adjudicating disputed issues. And hopes for the spread of freedom foundered against the tragic insistence of the rulers of the Soviet Union upon retaining the totalitarian regime inherited from their 1917 revolution and upon spreading its grasp over the neighboring peoples unwillingly subjected to them by the war. Millions of Europeans, therefore, lived in a state of perpetual tension, torn between the desire to attain a greater degree of liberty and the danger that a struggle might touch off a renewal of large-scale fighting.

The situation was most extreme in the large areas of Eastern Europe subjected to Soviet control against the will of the populace. The countries annexed to the Soviet Union — Latvia, Lithuania, Estonia, and part

of Finland — were doomed to impotence. The power of the Soviet state simply spread across the region and crushed all existing institutions. There people learned to live without hope or delusions.

Hope survived for a time in the satellite states governed by puppets. Often the Communist parties there contained individuals who sincerely expected that a democratic, humane form of socialism would evolve after the end of the crisis of postwar reconstruction. In some of these countries they ruled in coalition with non-Communist elements who shared those hopes. And the mass of farmers and laborers who had suffered from exploitation for decades also assumed that the state ultimately would serve their interests.

But as the years went by these dreams faded to leave the subject population despondent or desperate. Utopia came no closer and one crisis followed another. A succession of spontaneous uprisings and protests expressed popular resentment. East Germany in 1953, Hungary in 1956, and Czechoslovakia in 1968 were the dramatic eruptions; lesser resentments simmered beneath the surface. All were ruthlessly suppressed, for behind the local gendarmerie was the colossal might of the Soviet Red Army.

The truth was that the individuals or even small states simply lacked the power to make their will felt against the invader; and the United Nations was helpless. Those who did not wish to accept life under the Communist terms imposed by Russia had only one alternative — flight. After the Hungarian tragedy fully 200,000 fugitives voted with their feet by departing. Most of those who escaped found homes in neighboring countries, and especially in Austria, Switzerland,

and Germany. But occasional groups fought their way to the United States. Americans, unable to help the invaded lands out of fear of spreading the conflagration, felt the obligation at least to provide sanctuary for some of the victims.

The cold war had an ideological as well as a political aspect. The battle raged in the minds of men as well as around the diplomats' tables and on the battlefronts; and people who judged freedom in the American pattern preferable both to the oppression behind the Iron Curtain and the detached neutrality of Western Europe struggled to reach the New World. Little groups of Poles, Lithuanians, Latvians, and Yugoslavs — often officials of governments ousted by the Communists — settled in America; larger numbers of Hungarians, Germans, and Czechs in time joined them. In 1954, representatives of these groups formed the Assembly of Captive European Nations to keep alive the cause of these countries.

The Soviet Union felt the force of this attraction most directly. Some members of the Russian emigré colony in Paris, among them Aleksandr Kerensky and Boris Nicolaevsky, early made the decision to come to the United States. In 1944 Viktor A. Kravchenko, an important official in the Soviet secret service, defected and in his book, *I Chose Freedom,* revealed the slavery of Stalin's labor camps and the oppression that extended through all levels of society in the U.S.S.R. In time the number of defectors grew and culminated in 1968 with the arrival of Svetlana Alliluyeva, the daughter of the dictator Joseph Stalin, who added her own recollections of life in the Kremlin to the growing exposé literature.

The reaction of European intellectuals was significant. Some, committed to antibourgeois and anti-American attitudes, were unwilling to credit these revelations. Jean-Paul Sartre and his followers, attracted by the decisive cathartic violence of revolution, whether executed by blond warriors from the north or by muscular Slavs from the east or simply by criminals, insistently denied that the workers' paradise had taken a wrong turn. Until Khrushchev revealed the full evidence of Stalin's crimes, they refused to admit that Communist rule rested upon terror and upon the deliberate manipulation of anti-Semitism. And when denial was no longer possible, the pro-Soviet writers treated the revelations as proof of a wholesome reform. The twists and turns of their apologetics poisoned the atmosphere and persuaded a sensitive writer like Nina Berberova to leave the Old World for the New.

The conflict reached to Asia and Latin America also. China had suffered from instability, misrule, and foreign invasion for decades, before the Communists established their control in 1949. The new regime ruthlessly consolidated its position by suppressing dissent, and escape was rarely possible except at moments of extreme pressure. After 1958, for instance, a combination of political oppression and famine forced substantial numbers to flee to the nearest exit at Hong Kong. The influx threatened to create a crisis in that city and put pressure on Washington to admit some refugees as immigrants.

The problem was even closer to home after Fidel Castro seized power in Cuba. The United States had made the Cuban Revolution possible by cutting off aid to the Batista dictatorship; and Americans at first wel-

*Difficult as the transitional years were, few of
Europe's tired and poor chose to return to the famine
and oppression that they had originally fled. Millions
immigrated; thousands emigrated. And over the
decades the statue's beacon continued to shed its
powerful light across both oceans.*

comed the change. But Castro soon disregarded his promise to hold early elections. Instead of liberalizing the political system he set a totalitarian course and went further in the use of terror than his predecessor had. Since the immigration laws did not exclude natives of the Western Hemisphere, the result was a massive migration across the narrow channel to Florida. Ultimately, almost 500,000 Cubans found homes in the United States.

Continuing involvement in these events led to a reconsideration of American policy. In 1965, a new statute discarded the biased national origins quota system and put all applicants for admission on an equal basis. The new law also made special provision for political refugees, recognizing the continuing obligation of the Republic to the victims of repression in every part of the world.

In 1950, when they still arrived mainly by ship, immigrants could yet look beyond the great statue to see the city rise "magically out of the water, tall and narrow like a Gothic cathedral." Two decades later they were more likely to touch down in an international airport, quite similar to airports anywhere else in the world. It took more imagination in 1970 to make out the magic of what lay beyond.

Just about a century had then passed since Bartholdi, smarting from the French defeat, had turned his thoughts to a monument to liberty in New York harbor. The intellectual and emotional needs of the moment drew his creative energies in that direction; and those needs grew out of a persistent image Europeans had long held of the distinctive society that had developed in the New World.

But the United States was not quite what Europe thought it was; hence the awkwardness with which Americans accepted the Statue of Liberty. The people whom Bartholdi curiously observed were neither wilderness philosophers nor noble republican heroes. They were simple men and women engaged in the ordinary business of earning a living, making homes, and pursuing happiness in their own fashion. But they did have a distinctive relationship to the world beyond their borders for they were almost all immigrants or the descendants of immigrants and their whole history had been an uncovering of the meaning of liberty.

Freedom they had discovered not from books of theories but from experience, first in its implications for man's conscience, then in its relevance to the forms of government, and in time in its significance for satisfying economic and social wants. Without plan or design, they had groped through the generations for ways in which they could live together and help one another, while expanding each person's capacities and while imposing no unnecessary restraints. A century after Bartholdi's visit, they were far from having reached the goal, but they were closer to it than ever before and closer also than most nations had ever been.

And throughout this long, often confused, venture they had rarely viewed their efforts in narrow parochial terms. Despite the occasional temptations of an escape to isolation, they usually remembered what the continuing flow of immigrants would not let them forget, that their cause had significance for all mankind. The torch kindled above Bedloe's Island drew its fuel from the labor of the American people but it cast light abroad to illuminate a way to liberty for all men.

IMMIGRANT
MEMOIRS

THE AMERICAN DREAM

J. Hector St. John Crèvecoeur's Letters from an American Farmer *is perhaps the earliest complete description of "the American, this new man." Born in France, Crèvecoeur traveled extensively throughout the colonies before settling in New York in the early 1770's. From his farm in Orange County, he recorded an impassioned and optimistic vision of America's potentialities.*

We are the most perfect society now existing in the world. Here man is free as he ought to be; nor is this pleasing equality so transitory as many others are. Many ages will not see the shores of our great lakes replenished with inland nations, nor the unknown bounds of North America entirely peopled. Who can tell how far it extends? Who can tell the millions of men whom it will feed and contain? for no European foot has as yet travelled half the extent of this mighty continent!

. . . whence came all these people? they are a mixture of English, Scotch, Irish, French, Dutch, Germans, and Swedes. From this promiscuous breed, that race now called Americans have arisen. . . .

In this great American asylum, the poor of Europe have by some means met together, and in consequence of various causes; to what purpose should they ask one another what countrymen they are? Alas, two thirds of them had no country. Can a wretch who wanders about, who works and starves, whose life is a continual scene of sore affliction or pinching penury; can that man call England or any other kingdom his country? A country that had no bread for him, whose fields procured him no harvest, who met with nothing but the frowns of the rich, the severity of the laws, with jails and punishments; who owned not a single foot of the extensive surface of this planet? No! urged by a variety of motives, here they came. Every thing has tended to regenerate them; new laws, a new mode of living, a new social system; here they are become men: in Europe they were as so many useless plants, wanting vegetative mould, and refreshing showers; they withered, and were mowed down by want, hunger, and war; but now by the power of transplantation, like all other plants they have taken root and flourished! Formerly they were not numbered in any civil lists of their country, except in those of the poor; here they rank as citizens. By what invisible power has this surprising metamorphosis been performed? By that of the laws and that of their industry. The laws, the indulgent laws, protect them as they arrive, stamping on them the symbol of adoption. . . .

. . . What then is the American, this new man? He is either an European, or the descendant of an European, hence that strange mixture of blood, which you will find in no other country. I could point out to you a family whose grandfather was an Englishman, whose wife was Dutch, whose son married a French woman, and whose present four sons have now four wives of different nations. *He* is an American, who leaving behind him all his ancient prejudices and manners, receives new ones from the new mode of life he has embraced, the new government he obeys, and the new rank he holds. He becomes an American by being received in the broad lap of our great *Alma Mater*. Here individuals of all nations are melted into a new race of men, whose labours and posterity will one day cause great changes in the world. Americans are the western pilgrims, who are carrying along with them that great mass of arts, sciences, vigour, and industry which began long since in the east; they will finish the great circle. The Americans were

In this 1886 engraving, New Yorkers throng lower Broadway to watch a parade celebrating the dedication of the Statue of Liberty

once scattered all over Europe; here they are incorporated into one of the finest systems of population which has ever appeared, and which will hereafter become distinct by the power of the different climates they inhabit. The American ought therefore to love this country much better than that wherein either he or his forefathers were born. Here the rewards of his industry follow with equal steps the progress of his labour; his labour is founded on the basis of nature, *self-interest;* can it want a stronger allurement? Wives and children, who before in vain demanded of him a morsel of bread, now, fat and frolicsome, gladly help their father to clear those fields whence exuberant crops are to arise to feed and to clothe them all; without any part being claimed, either by a despotic prince, a rich abbot, or a mighty lord. . . . The American is a new man, who acts upon new principles; he must therefore entertain new ideas, and form new opinions. From involuntary idleness, servile dependence, penury, and useless labour, he has passed to toils of a very different nature, rewarded by ample subsistence. — This is an American.

J. HECTOR ST. JOHN CRÈVECOEUR
Letters from an American Farmer, 1782

To Gjert G. Hovland, a Norwegian pioneer, America was the land of opportunity — provided one was willing to work hard. In a letter written in 1838 to a friend back home, he gives judicious and practical advice to the prospective immigrant.

THE VOYAGE
OVER

I cannot neglect my duty to write, reminded as I am of my old native country Norway and my friends there. Since my childhood, I have been very deficient in education, but as I hope that this letter will reach you safely, I take occasion to write with the hope that those who have more intelligence than I will take my humble contribution in good part. More particularly, this is addressed to you whom I came to know as a faithful friend. I know that this year reports on America are not lacking in Norway, as far as they get through; but they differ according to everybody's understanding and insight.

I suppose that people are emigrating in great numbers from Norway now, and every emigrant has a different attitude. Many have arrived here who knew Norway under straitened circumstances, and looking back, they see only the burdens they have cast off and feel happy in their emigration, especially for their children. But those, on the other hand, who grew up in the nurture of pious parents and who always enjoyed earthly happiness, will find sorrow and regret if they expect God to supply them a paradise here without the necessity of working. Everyone who leaves Norway with this fond hope is deceiving himself thoroughly. Anyone who wants to make good here has to work, just as in all other places in the world. But here everything is better rewarded. This fact repels many people, though anyone with common sense ought to know that in time life rewards each as he deserves. Therefore, it seems to me all who take a notion to visit this country had better consider the matter carefully before they leave their homes, nor should they enter upon the venture frivolously or intoxicated by greed for material things. This applies especially to people who vacillate and lack firmness.

Since the length of the journey makes the trip here rather expensive, those who want to manage on their own without contracting any debts must be prepared to pay from seventy to eighty specie dollars for every adult and half that amount for children, besides the price of provisions. When they arrive here, they find that no land is available in Illinois, though there is some farther west; but it requires money and patience to get there. The land around here that has enough woodland has been bought up and is inhabited. We have an unbelievable amount of vast grass plains (savannas) that extend for many miles with the most marvelous grazing for the animals imaginable. As much hay as anyone could desire may be mowed with little trouble. Surely no sensible man could wish for a better place. But even so, many people are dissatisfied with everything, especially those who are full of ambition. They bother others with their regrets and pine for the ceremonies and compliments of the fine world. We set little store by that sort of thing here. We who are accustomed to work since childhood feel that this is Canaan when we consider the fertile soil that without manuring brings forth such rich crops of everything. Norway cannot be compared to America any more than a desert can be compared to a garden in full bloom. . . .

I am glad that I came here, though things have not always gone according to my wish since I left New York, where I settled at first. . . . I have bought 160 acres of land which lies in the shape of a quadrangle and is two miles in circumference. The land here is beautiful, but the winter is long with a piercing kind of cold that I have never known the like of before. Moreover, the heat is so intense that sometimes it is difficult to bear long spells of it during our seasons of hard work. Therefore, I do not advise anyone in Norway who is making a good living there to leave it, particularly not older people, for they will not be able to get along. Since they cannot learn the language and are ill suited for hard work, everything will displease them here. But unattached persons will be able to better themselves. If I live long enough, I plan to visit you some time.

The Almighty Lord will be with you all in your several undertakings. I hope you are well — I am myself well, God be praised.

GJERT G. HOVLAND
Letter to a Friend, 1838

Whatever it was they sought to escape by emigrating to the New World — economic hardship, religious persecution, or political oppression — the vast majority of nineteenth-century immigrants first had to endure the treacherous Atlantic crossing to reach their goal. An anonymous Norwegian immigrant describes his shipboard experiences in the confined space below decks known as the steerage.

The crossing from Liverpool was a bad one. We went on board our ship on October 13 and left on the morning of the fourteenth, but we did not get any farther than to an anchorage about half a Norwegian mile from Liverpool, where we were forced to stay until the eighteenth because cholera had been raging on a few ships that left about the same time as we did. On one of the ships which had left a couple of days earlier 125 persons had died, but on board my ship only twelve persons died during the voyage, and a child was born three days before we reached the shore of America.

The crossing was terrible. Three days after we had left land, we had a frightful storm, and during the night we lost the mainmast and the foremast, so that later we had to get along by means of jury-rigged masts and sails. Many of the berths on the lower deck collapsed, and water poured down through the hatchways so that coffers, trunks, sacks, and all kinds of loose objects floated around in the water and were in great part broken against the sides of the ship because of the terribly heavy sea. That many provisions were spoilt and clothes and the like damaged by the water is easy to understand. This storm lasted two days and two nights, and during this time we had to go both hungry and thirsty, since we could not manage to prepare anything in the galley where everybody was supposed to cook his own food. We could not get any fresh water either.

In the galley there was a large stove; but as there were always a lot of people who wanted to cook, the only law that prevailed here was club law. The strongest and most aggressive could always, although with difficulty, get something cooked, while the weaker and more timid got nothing or had to content themselves with being the last in line, at the risk of having their pots, with half-cooked food, thrown off the fire when the stronger were pleased to come back.

Fights and quarrels were daily occurrences, and the company had done nothing to make sure that everybody was treated justly and the promises that had been made were kept. In Christiania [now Oslo] we were promised all sorts of things — for instance, that the food would be excellent. With regard to this, let me give you just one small illustration of the way these promises were kept. Every Saturday we got our provisions; they consisted of six or seven biscuits, about three eighths of a pound of brown sugar, a little wheat flour, some rice and groats, and ten pounds of beef; the meat was to last for the whole passage, but most of it was bone. What kind of food do you think one could prepare with this, especially since we got so little water for cooking that we might very well have used up all of it at once?

At our departure we were promised a sufficient amount of fresh water, but we got so little that we had to be satisfied with making a small cup of tea in the morning and cooking a little porridge later in the day. As for getting water to quench our thirst, that was out of the question. We could not make any broth with the meat we had been given but had to cut it into small pieces and cook it with the porridge. I used the wheat flour I had been given for baking a small cake on Sunday; and being fairly strong and aggressive I shoved back at people and succeeded in getting this holiday treat for myself. Otherwise, our daily fare was the small cup of tea I have mentioned and a biscuit in the morning and porridge for dinner. For supper we had nothing, and I can truthfully say that never . . . have I suffered more, nor do I believe that people can suffer more than . . . on [these] overpraised ships. . . .

From the knowledge I have of America now, I think I shall never suffer such want anywhere as I did on board the ship, where we were so starved and thirsty that I thought I should never set foot on land again. God be praised, during the crossing I did not suffer from any other illness than hunger and thirst. From what I have already said, you may imagine how my life has been during this time, for I went on board on October 13 and did not get ashore till November 28.

ANONYMOUS
Letter to his Mother, c. 1853

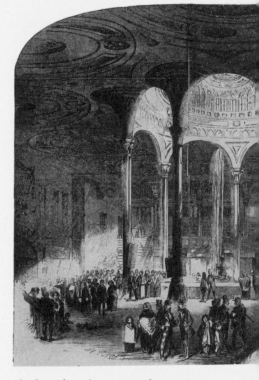

An interior view of Castle Garden as an immigration center — more elegant than accurate

Those Europeans who survived the rigors of passage could look forward to the promise of a better life in America. But African "immigrants" who somehow managed to survive their involuntary voyage faced a lifetime of slavery. In this excerpt from his autobiography Charles Ball, a slave born in late eighteenth-century Maryland, relates the life story of an African-born slave he met on a Carolina plantation. Although the language is not that of an uneducated slave — since Ball did not do the actual writing — the experiences he describes are.

About a month after I came to the [neighboring African] village we were alarmed one morning, just at break of day, by the horrible uproar caused by mingled shouts of men, and blows given with heavy sticks upon large wooden drums. The village was surrounded by enemies, who attacked us with clubs, long wooden spears, and bows and arrows. After fighting for more than an hour, those who were not fortunate enough to run away, were made prisoners. It was not the object of our enemies to kill; they wished to take us alive, and sell us as slaves. I was knocked down by a heavy blow of a club, and when I recovered from the stupor that followed, I found myself tied fast with the long rope that I had brought from the desert, and in which I had formerly led the camels of my masters.

We were immediately led away from this village, through the forest, and were compelled to travel all day, as fast as we could walk. We had nothing to eat on this journey, but a small quantity of grain, taken with ourselves. . . . We travelled three weeks in the woods — sometimes without any path at all; and arrived one day at a large river, with a rapid current. . . .

. . . [We] formed a raft, upon which we all placed ourselves, and descended the river for three days, when we came in sight of what appeared to me the most wonderful object in the world; this was a large ship, at anchor, in the river. When our raft came near the ship, the white people — for such they were on board — assisted to take us on deck, and the logs were suffered to float down the river.

I had never seen white people before; and they appeared to me the ugliest creatures in the world. The persons who brought us down the river received payment for us of the people in the ship, in various articles, of which I remember that a keg of liquor, and some yards of blue and red cotton cloth, were the principal. At the time we came into this ship, she was full of black people, who were all confined in a dark and low place, in irons. The women were in irons as well as the men.

About twenty persons were seized in our village, at the time I was; and amongst these were three children, so young that they were not able to walk, or to eat any hard substance. The mothers of these children had brought them all the way with them; and had them in their arms when we were taken on board this ship.

When they put us in irons, to be sent to our place of confinement in the ship, the men who fastened the irons on these mothers, took the children out of their hands, and threw them over the side of the ship, into the water. When this was done, two of the women leaped overboard after the children — the third was already confined by a chain to another woman, and could not get into the water, but in struggling to disengage herself she broke her arm, and died a few days after, of a fever. One of the two women who were in the river, was carried down by the weight of her irons, before she could be rescued; but the other was taken up by some men in a boat, and brought on board. This woman threw herself overboard one night, when we were at sea.

The weather was very hot, whilst we lay in the river, and many of us died every day; but the number brought on board greatly exceeded those who died, and at the end of two weeks the place in which we were confined was so full that no one could lie down; and we were obliged to sit all the time, for the room was not high enough for us to stand. When our prison would hold no more, the ship sailed down the river, and on the second day after she sailed, I heard the roaring of the ocean, as it dashed against her sides.

After we had been at sea some days, the irons were removed from the women, and they were permitted to go upon deck; but whenever the wind blew high, they were driven down amongst us.

We had nothing to eat but yams, which were thrown amongst us at random — and of these we had scarcely enough to support life. More than one-third of us died on the passage; and when we arrived at Charleston, I was not able to stand. It was more than a week after I left the ship, before I could straighten my limbs. I was bought by a trader, with several others; brought up the country and sold to our present master: I have been here five years.

CHARLES BALL
A Narrative of the Life and Adventures of Charles Ball, a Black Man, 1837

FIRST IMPRESSIONS

Carl Schurz was forced to flee his native Germany at the age of nineteen, after serving as an officer in the abortive 1848 uprising. The young revolutionary — who was to become a brigadier general during the Civil War and later U.S. Senator from Missouri and Secretary of the Interior — describes his earliest impressions of American democracy.

During our sojourn in Philadelphia [in the 1850's] our social intercourse was necessarily limited. But I availed myself of every opportunity of talking with people of various classes and of thus informing myself about their ways of thinking, their hopes and apprehensions, their prejudices and their sympathies. At the same time I industriously studied the political history and institutions of the country, and, as to current events and their significance, my newspaper reading soon went beyond the columns of the *Ledger.* The impressions I received were summed up in a letter which at that period I wrote to my friend, Miss Malwida von Meysenburg. I had long forgotten it when years afterwards it turned up in her "Memoirs of an Idealist," an exceedingly interesting book which has so well held its place in literature that but recently, more than a quarter of a century after its first appearance, a new edition has been printed and widely read.

In that letter I described how the European idealists, as I knew them in the old world, would at first be startled, if not shocked, by the aspect of a really free people, — a democracy in full operation on a large scale, — the most contradictory tendencies and antagonistic movements openly at work, side by side, or against one another, enlightenment and stupid bigotry, good citizenship and lawlessness, benevolent and open-handed public spirit and

*Immigrants crowd a passenger ship
bound for the New World*

rapacious greed, democracy and slavery, independent spirit and subserviency to party despotism and to predominant public opinion — all this in bewildering confusion. The newly arrived European democrat, having lived in a world of theories and imaginings without having had any practical experience of a democracy at work, beholding it for the first time, asks himself: "Is this really a people living in freedom? Is this the realization of my ideal?" He is puzzled and perplexed, until it dawns upon him that, in a condition of real freedom, man manifests himself, not as he ought to be, but as he is, with all his bad as well as his good qualities, instincts, and impulses: with all his attributes of strength as well as all his weaknesses; that this, therefore, is not an ideal state, but simply a state in which the forces of good have a free field as against the forces of evil, and in which the victories of virtue, of enlightenment, and of progress are not achieved by some power or agency outside of the people, for their benefit, but *by* the people themselves.

Such victories of the forces of good may be slow in being accomplished, but they will be all the more thorough and durable in their effects, because they will be the product of the people's own thought and effort. The people may commit follies or mistakes ever so grievous, but having committed those follies or mistakes themselves and upon their own responsibility, they will be apt to profit by their own experience. If those mistakes were rectified by some superior authority, the people would be apt to run into the same mistakes again. If the people are left to correct the mistakes themselves, they will more surely progress in wisdom as well as in the sense of responsibility. Whatever stands upon the bottom of the popular intelligence, stands upon far firmer ground than that which rests merely upon superior authority.

"Here in America," I wrote to my friend, "you can see daily how little a people needs to be governed. There are governments, but no masters; there are governors, but they are only commissioners, agents. What there is here of great institutions of learning, of churches, of great commercial institutions, lines of communication, etc., almost always owes its existence, not to official authority, but to the spontaneous co-operation of private citizens. Here you witness the productiveness of freedom. You see a magnificent church — a voluntary association of private persons has founded it; an orphan asylum built of marble — a wealthy citizen has erected it; a university — some rich men have left a large bequest for educational purposes, which serves as a capital stock, and the university then lives, so to speak, almost on subscriptions; and so on without end. We learn here how superfluous is the action of governments concerning a multitude of things in which in Europe it is deemed absolutely indispensable, and how the freedom to do something awakens the desire to do it."

Although I am well aware of its crudities of expression, its inaccuracies of statement, and of the incompleteness of its presentation of American conditions, I quote this letter because it portrays fairly well the workings of the mind of a young man who has been suddenly transplanted from the Old World — its ways of thinking, its traditional views of life, its struggles, illusions, and ideals — into a new world where he witnesses the operation of elementary forces in open daylight, and the realities of free government in undisguised exhibition.

CARL SCHURZ
The Reminiscences of Carl Schurz, 1907

The high expectations of immigrants who sought to make their fortunes by buying land in America were often cruelly shattered. This anonymous Welshman found almost nothing to his liking in the Kansas of 1870.

After I landed in New York I came to the conclusion that the less one travels in this country the better off one is. It would have been better had I not left New York which is the best place that the Yankees have here. But some people persuaded me that the further west the better it is. I could not believe this but I gave it a try during the winter which was the best time, as I was out of work. I am sending you newspapers from the people selling the land here so that you can judge for yourselves. But beware of catching the American fever when reading them. You can say before starting to read them that every word is untrue. What enticed me to Kansas was to get a little land but by now the amount of land I expect to get is six feet by two feet. The people in the Old Country do not have the vaguest idea what sort of place America is. . . . Those who have lived here ten years look more like Indians than Welshmen. They have not been able in ten years to save enough money to build a house of any kind. They live in holes in the ground something like the potato-caches that you see in Wales. The sight of them is enough to put anyone off who is thinking of farming in America. The truth is that the land in Kansas is expensive for nothing. Many think that all of the land here is good but that is a great mistake. There is land in almost every state which is not worth having even if you got it for nothing. . . .

. . . The government gives twenty miles of land to the railroad companies on either side of the line and of course everyone in these new states wants to be as near to the iron road as they can and when a new railroad is being built the land sharks buy up the land straightaway from the company. And remember that the Yankees here are sharp and they always pick the best and they can perhaps put down the money. And then along come the Welsh and they  have what is left and with perhaps ten years to pay for it and having bought it perhaps quite cheaply. The next task will be to entice the simple Welshman to buy land from them which belongs to the railroad company. They do the same thing with government land if they see that some place is likely to be settled. They are there by the hundreds picking the best land for about two dollars and selling it again for perhaps fifty dollars. Many would think from the papers in the Old Country that all you have to do is to come to a state and settle there, that the land is to be had for practically nothing, but this is completely wrong. There is plenty of land in every state hardly even touched. You would think that it belonged to no one but try to get a bit of it and you straightaway find that it belongs to a land shark and it is the same all over the country. Thousands of Americans have made their fortunes selling land. . . . Well, you say, what sort of place is America for a poor man or a working man? It is a poor, yes, a very poor place here, especially the farther west you go. One could do better in New York or Pennsylvania if only one could get regular work, which is almost as difficult, if not more so, than in Manchester, due to the weather and the lack of materials. A man can hardly keep himself with one thing and another. He does not work half his time and there are too many workmen here by half and as everything is so dear and work so scarce it is a poor place for a man without money.

ANONYMOUS
Letter to his Brother and Sister, 1870

Despite the hardships many immigrants suffered in America, few of them ever forgot their first awe-inspiring glimpse of the Statue of Liberty, symbol of the nation's promise. Edward Corsi, who later became commissioner of the immigrant processing center at Ellis Island, recalls the wonder, excitement, and apprehension of a ten-year-old Italian boy's first contact with America.

My first impressions of the new world will always remain etched in my memory, particularly that hazy October morning [in 1907] when I first saw Ellis Island. The steamer *Florida*, fourteen days out of Naples, filled to capacity with sixteen hundred natives of Italy, had weathered one of the worst storms in our captain's memory; and glad we were, both children and grown-ups, to leave the open sea and come at last through the Narrows into the Bay.

My mother, my stepfather, my brother Giuseppe, and my two sisters, Liberta and Helvetia, all of us together, happy that we had come through the storm safely, clustered on the foredeck for fear of separation and looked with wonder on this miraculous land of our dreams.

Giuseppe and I held tightly to stepfather's hands, while Liberta and Helvetia clung to mother. Passengers all about us were crowding against the rail. Jabbered conversation, sharp cries, laughs and cheers — a steadily rising din filled the air. Mothers and fathers lifted up the babies so that they too could see, off to the left, the Statue of Liberty.

I looked at that statue with a sense of bewilderment, half doubting its reality. Looming shadowy through the mist, it brought silence to the decks of the *Florida*. This symbol of America — this enormous expression of what we had all been taught was the inner meaning of this new country we were coming to — inspired awe in the hopeful immigrants. Many older persons among us, burdened with a thousand memories of what they were leaving behind, had been openly weeping ever since we entered the narrower waters on our final approach toward the unknown. Now somehow steadied, I suppose, by the concreteness of the symbol of America's freedom, they dried their tears.

Directly in front of the *Florida*, half visible in the faintly-colored haze, rose a second and even greater challenge to the imagination.

"Mountains!" I cried to Giuseppe. "Look at them!"

"They're strange," he said, "why don't they have snow on them?" He was craning his neck and standing on tiptoe to stare at the New York skyline.

Stepfather looked toward the skyscrapers, and, smiling, assured us that they were not mountains but buildings — "the highest buildings in the world."

On every side the harbor offered its marvels: tugs, barges, sloops, lighters, sluggish freighters and giant ocean liners — all moving in different directions, managing, by what seemed to us a miracle, to dart in and out and up and down without colliding with one another. They spoke to us through the varied sounds of their whistles, and the *Florida* replied with a deep echoing voice. Bells clanged through our ship, precipitating a new flurry among our fellow-passengers. Many of these people had come from provinces far distant from ours, and were shouting to one another in dialects strange to me. Everything combined to increase our excitement, and we rushed from deck to deck, fearful lest we miss the smallest detail of the spectacle.

Finally the *Florida* veered to the left, turning northward into the Hud-

Newcomers at the Battery are met by Union Army recruiting officers who offer inducements for enlistment

147

son River, and now the incredible buildings of lower Manhattan came very close to us.

The officers of the ship, mighty and unapproachable beings they seemed to me, went striding up and down the decks shouting orders and directions and driving the immigrants before them. Scowling and gesturing, they pushed and pulled the passengers, herding us into separate groups as though we were animals. A few moments later we came to our dock, and the long journey was over.

EDWARD CORSI
In the Shadow of Liberty, 1935

Born in a Russian ghetto in 1881, the descendant of generations of persecuted Jews, Mary Antin entered public school in a Boston slum at the age of twelve. In The Promised Land, *she describes her joyous odyssey from immigrant to American.*

Fond farewells at the dock in a European port

What the child thinks and feels is a reflection of the hopes, desires, and purposes of the parents who brought him overseas, no matter how precocious and independent the child may be. Your immigrant inspectors will tell you what poverty the foreigner brings in his baggage, what want in his pockets. Let the overgrown boy of twelve, reverently drawing his letters in the baby class, testify to the noble dreams and high ideals that may be hidden beneath the greasy caftan of the immigrant. . . .

Father himself conducted us to school. He would not have delegated that mission to the President of the United States. He had awaited the day with impatience equal to mine, and the visions he saw as he hurried us over the sun-flecked pavements transcended all my dreams. Almost his first act on landing on American soil, three years before, had been his application for naturalization. . . . and at the earliest moment allowed by the law, he became a citizen of the United States. It is true that he had left home in search of bread for his hungry family, but he went blessing the necessity that drove him to America. The boasted freedom of the New World meant to him far more than the right to reside, travel, and work wherever he pleased; it meant the freedom to speak his thoughts, to throw off the shackles of superstition, to test his own fate, unhindered by political or religious tyranny. He was only a young man when he landed — thirty-two; and most of his life he had been held in leading-strings [a state of dependence]. He was hungry for his untasted manhood.

Three years passed in sordid struggle and disappointment. He was not prepared to make a living even in America, where the day laborer eats wheat instead of rye. . . . In business, nothing prospered with him. Some fault of hand or mind or temperament led him to failure where other men found success. Wherever the blame for his disabilities be placed, he reaped their bitter fruit. "Give me bread!" he cried to America. "What will you do to earn it?" the challenge came back. And he found that he was master of no art, of no trade; that even his precious learning was of no avail. . . .

So it was with a heart full of longing and hope that my father led us to school on that first day. He took long strides in his eagerness, the rest of us running and hopping to keep up.

At last [we] stood around the teacher's desk; and my father, in his impos-

sible English, gave us over in her charge, with some broken word of his hopes for us that his swelling heart could no longer contain. . . .

. . . This foreigner, who brought his children to school as if it were an act of consecration, who regarded the teacher of the primer class with reverence, who spoke of visions, like a man inspired, in a common school-room, was not like other aliens, who brought their children in dull obedience to the law; was not like the native fathers, who brought their unmanageable boys, glad to be relieved of their care. I think Miss Nixon [the teacher] guessed what my father's best English could not convey. I think she divined that by the simple act of delivering our school certificates to her he took possession of America. . . .

How long would you say, wise reader, it takes to make an American? By the middle of my second year in school I had reached the sixth grade. When, after the Christmas holidays, we began to study the life of Washington, running through a summary of the Revolution, and the early days of the Republic, it seemed to me that all my reading and study had been idle until then. The reader, the arithmetic, the song book, that had so fascinated me until now, became suddenly sober exercise books. . . . I could not pronounce the name of George Washington without a pause. Never had I prayed, never had I chanted the songs of David, never had I called upon the Most Holy, in such utter reverence and worship as I repeated the simple sentences of my child's story of the patriot. I gazed with adoration at the portraits of George and Martha Washington, till I could see them with my eyes shut. . . .

. . . George Washington, who died long before I was born, was like a king in greatness, and he and I were Fellow Citizens. There was a great deal about Fellow Citizens in the patriotic literature we read at this time; and I knew from my father how he was a Citizen, through the process of naturalization, and how I also was a citizen, by virtue of my relation to him. Undoubtedly I was a Fellow Citizen, and George Washington was another. It thrilled me to realize what sudden greatness had fallen on me; and at the same time it sobered me, as with a sense of responsibility. I strove to conduct myself as befitted a Fellow Citizen. . . .

What more could America give a child? Ah, much more! As I read how the patriots planned the Revolution, and the women gave their sons to die in battle, and the heroes led to victory, and the rejoicing people set up the Republic, it dawned on me gradually what was meant by *my country*. . . .

Where had been my country until now? What flag had I loved? What heroes had I worshipped? The very names of these things had been unknown to me. Well I knew that Polotzk [a Russian ghetto] was not my country. It was *goluth*—exile. . . . We knew what it was to be Jews in exile, from the spiteful treatment we suffered at the hands of the smallest urchin who crossed himself. . . . But the story of the Exodus was not history to me in the sense that the story of the American Revolution was. It was more like a glorious myth, a belief in which had the effect of cutting me off from the actual world, by linking me with a world of phantoms. . . . In very truth we were a people without a country. Surrounded by mocking foes and detractors, it was difficult for me to realize the persons of my people's heroes or the events in which they moved. . . . For the conditions of our civil life did not permit us to cultivate a spirit of nationalism. The freedom of worship that was grudgingly granted . . . by no means included the right to set up openly any ideal of a Hebrew State, any hero other than the Czar. . . . As to our future, we Jews in Polotzk had no national expectations; only a lifeworn dreamer here and there hoped to die in Palestine. . . .

So it came to pass that we did not know what *my country* could mean to a man. And as we had no country, so we had no flag to love. It was by no far-fetched symbolism that the banner of the House of Romanoff became the emblem of our latter-day bondage in our eyes. Even a child would know how to hate the flag that we were forced, on pain of severe penalties, to hoist above our housetops, in celebration of the advent of one of our oppressors. And as it was with country and flag, so it was with heroes of war. We hated the uniform of the soldier, to the last brass button. On the person of a Gentile, it was the symbol of tyranny; on the person of a Jew, it was the emblem of shame.

So a little Jewish girl in Polotzk was apt to grow up hungry-minded and empty-hearted; and if, still in her outreaching youth, she was set down in a land of outspoken patriotism, she was likely to love her new country with a great love, and to embrace its heroes in a great worship. Naturalization, with us Russian Jews, may mean more than the adoption of the immigrant by America. It may mean the adoption of America by the immigrant.

MARY ANTIN
The Promised Land, 1912

Constantine Panunzio — penniless and ignorant of the English language when he arrived in Boston harbor — jumped ship in order to escape a sadistic captain and earn enough money to return to his native Italian town of Molfetta. The treatment the eighteen-year-old sailor experienced on land was typical of the reception many newcomers encountered in America's major cities at the turn of the century.

CULTURE SHOCK

Late in the evening of September 8, 1902, when the turmoil of the street traffic was subsiding, and the silence of the night was slowly creeping over the city, I took my sea chest, my sailor bag and all I had and set foot on American soil. I was in America. Of immigration laws I had not even a knowledge of their existence; of the English language I knew not a word; of friends I had none in Boston or elsewhere in America to whom I might turn for counsel or help. I had exactly fifty cents remaining out of a dollar which the captain had finally seen fit to give me. But as I was soon to earn money and return to Molfetta, I felt no concern.

. . . So the next morning bright and early . . . I started out in search of a job. I roamed about the streets, not knowing where or to whom to turn. That day and the next four days I had one loaf of bread each day for food and at night, not having money with which to purchase shelter, I stayed on the recreation pier on Commercial Street. One night, very weary and lonely, I lay upon a bench and soon dozed off into a light sleep. The next thing I knew I cried out in bitter pain and fright. A policeman had stolen up to me very quietly and with his club had dealt me a heavy blow upon the soles of my feet. He drove me away, and I think I cried; I cried my first American cry. What became of me that night I cannot say. And the next day and the next. . . . I just roamed aimlessly about the streets, between the Public Gardens with its flowers and the water-side, where I watched the children at play, even as I had played at the water's brink in old Molfetta.

Those first five days in America have left an impression upon my mind which can never be erased with the years, and which gives me a most profound sense of sympathy for immigrants as they arrive. . . .

So we went out to hunt our first job in America. For several mornings Louis [a French sailor Panunzio met in Boston] and I went to North Square, where there were generally a large number of men loitering in groups discussing all kinds of subjects, particularly the labor market. One morning . . . we saw a fat man coming toward us. "Buon giorno, padrone," said one of the men. "Padrone?" said I to myself. Now the word "padrone" in Italy is applied to a proprietor, generally a respectable man, at least one whose dress and appearance distinguish him as a man of means. This man not only showed no signs of good breeding in his face, but he was unshaven and dirty and his clothes were shabby. I could not quite understand how he could be called "padrone." However, I said nothing, first because I wanted to get back home, and second because I wanted to be polite when I was in *American* society!

The "padrone" came up to our group and began to wax eloquent and to gesticulate (both in Sicilian dialect) about the advantages of a certain job. I remember very clearly the points which he emphasized: "It is not very far, only twelve miles from Boston. For a few cents you can come back any time you wish. . . . The company has a 'shantee' in which you can sleep, and a 'storo' where you can buy your 'grosserie' all very cheap. 'Buona paga,'" he continued " (Good pay), $1.25 per day, and you only have to pay me fifty cents a week for having gotten you this 'gooda jobba.' I only do it to help you and because you are my countrymen. If you come back here at six o'clock to-night with your buddies, I myself will take you out."

The magnanimity of this man impressed Louis and me very profoundly; we looked at each other and said, "Wonderful!" We decided we would go; so at the appointed hour we returned to the very spot. About twenty men finally gathered there and we were led to North Station. There we took a train to some suburban place, the name of which I have never been able to learn. On reaching our destination we were taken to the "shantee" where we were introduced to two long open bunks filled with straw. These were to be our beds. The "storo" of which we had been told was at one end of the shanty. The next morning we were taken out to work. It was a sultry autumn day. The "peek" [pick] seemed to grow heavier at every stroke and the "shuvle" [shovel] wider and larger in its capacity to hold the gravel. The second day was no better than the first, and the third was worse than the second. The work was heavy and monotonous to Louis and myself especially, who had never been "contadini" [farm laborers] like the rest. The "padrone" whose magnanimity had so stirred us was little better than a brute. We began to do some simple figuring and discovered that when we had paid for our groceries at the "storo," for the privilege of sleeping in the shanty, and the fifty cents to the "padrone" for having been so condescending as to employ us, we would have nothing left but sore arms and backs. So on the afternoon of the third day Louis and I held a solemn conclave and decided to part company with "peek and shuvle," — for ever. We left, without receiving a cent of pay, of course.

CONSTANTINE M. PANUNZIO
The Soul of an Immigrant, 1969

For many immigrants, adjustment to American mores and values involved the sacrifice of older, deeply held ideals. Edward Bok, a Dutch immigrant who eventually became editor of the Ladies Home Journal, *recalls the lessons he learned in the streets of Boston in the 1870's.*

Immigrants aboard ship submit to vaccination by U.S. health officials

When I came to the United States as a lad of six, the most needful lesson for me, as a boy, was the necessity for thrift. I had been taught in my home across the sea that thrift was one of the fundamentals in a successful life. My family had come from a land (the Netherlands) noted for its thrift; but we had been in the United States only a few days before the realization came home strongly to my father and mother that they had brought their children to a land of waste.

Where the Dutchman saved, the American wasted. There was waste, and the most prodigal waste, on every hand. In every street-car and on every ferry-boat the floors and seats were littered with newspapers that had been read and thrown away or left behind. If I went to a grocery store to buy a peck of potatoes, and a potato rolled off the heaping measure, the grocery-man, instead of picking it up, kicked it into the gutter for the wheels of his wagon to run over. The butcher's waste filled my mother's soul with dismay. If I bought a scuttle of coal at the corner grocery, the coal that missed the scuttle, instead of being shovelled up and put back into the bin, was swept into the street. My young eyes quickly saw this; in the evening I gathered up the coal thus swept away, and during the course of a week I collected a scuttleful. The first time my mother saw the garbage pail of a family almost as poor as our own, with the wife and husband constantly complaining that they could not get along, she could scarcely believe her eyes. A half pan of hominy of the preceding day's breakfast lay in the pail next to a third of a loaf of bread. In later years, when I saw, daily, a scow loaded with the garbage of Brooklyn householders being towed through New York harbor out to sea, it was an easy calculation that what was thrown away in a week's time from Brooklyn homes would feed the poor of the Netherlands.

At school, I quickly learned that to "save money" was to be "stingy"; as a young man, I soon found that the American disliked the word "economy," and on every hand as plenty grew spending grew. There was literally nothing in American life to teach me thrift or economy; everything to teach me to spend and to waste.

I saw men who had earned good salaries in their prime, reach the years of incapacity as dependents. I saw families on every hand either living quite up to their means or beyond them; rarely within them. The more a man earned, the more he — or his wife — spent. I saw fathers and mothers and their children dressed beyond their incomes. The proportion of families who ran into debt was far greater than those who saved. . . .

As a Dutch boy, one of the cardinal truths taught me was that whatever was worth doing was worth doing well: that next to honesty came thoroughness as a factor in success. It was not enough that anything should be done: it was not done at all if it was not done well. I came to America to be taught exactly the opposite. The two infernal Americanisms "That's good enough" and "That will do" were early taught me, together with the maxim of quantity rather than quality.

EDWARD BOK
The Americanization of Edward Bok, 1920

Constantine Panunzio, the young Italian sailor whose bitter experience as a day laborer was previously described, remained in America and became a clergyman and social worker. He returned to Boston's North End in 1914 at the age of thirty to appraise his countrymen's adjustment to American life.

As I looked about me I said to myself: "Well, this is a real immigrant community, of which I have heard so much in the American world!" From the moment I first set foot in it, I began to be conscious of the tremendous difficulties which on the one hand confront America in her desire and efforts to assimilate immigrant groups; and which, on the other, are in the way of the immigrants themselves in their need, and often their desire, to become an integral part of the body American.

For one thing, here was a congestion the like of which I had never seen before. Within the narrow limits of one-half square mile were crowded together thirty-five thousand people, living tier upon tier, huddled together until the very heavens seemed to be shut out. These narrow alley-like streets of Old Boston were one mass of litter. The air was laden with soot and dirt. Ill odors arose from every direction. Here were no trees; no parks worthy of the name; no playgrounds other than the dirty streets for the children to play on; no birds to sing their songs; no flowers to waft their perfume; and only small strips of sky to be seen; while around the entire neighborhood like a mighty cordon, a thousand thousand wheels of commercial activity whirled incessantly day and night, making noises which would rack the sturdiest of nerves.

And who was responsible for this condition of things, for this crowding together? Were the immigrants alone to blame? Did they not occupy the very best tenements available, the moment they were erected and thrown open to them, even though at exorbitant rates?

Not only was all this true, but every sign of America seemed to have been systematically rooted out from this community as if with a ruthless purpose. Here still stood old Faneuil Hall, the Cradle of Liberty; here the old North Church still lifted its steeple as if reminding one of the part it had played in the Revolutionary War; . . . and here too, the spot where the Boston Tea Party . . . had taken place. But while these monuments stood like sentinels reminding one of what this neighborhood had once been, now every last vestige of America was gone! All the American churches, homes, clubs and other institutions which once had graced these streets were gone forever; gone to some more favorable spot in the uptown section of the city, leaving this community to work out its own destiny as best it could. There *were* churches here, to be sure, Catholic and Protestant and Jewish, but they were representative of other than America; they were under the leadership of men who, consciously or unconsciously, stood for other than American sentiments and ideals. In the homes and on the streets no English language was spoken save by the children; on the newsstands a paper in English could scarcely be found; here were scores if not hundreds of societies, national, provincial, local and sub-local, in which English was not usually spoken and in which other than American interests were largely represented. There were schools also in which the future citizens of America were taught in a language other than English. Here, when on a certain patriotic occasion, the American flag was raised a moment sooner than another flag, the person responsible for such a "crime" was nearly rushed out of the community. Above the stores . . . the signs were mainly in a foreign language. In a word, here was a community in America in which there was not a sign of the best of American life. . . .

Nor was this the whole story. Not only were all the constructive forces of American society absent from this community, but also some of its very worst features seemed to have been systematically poured into the neighborhood to prey upon the life of the people in their all too apparent helplessness. Here within this half mile square were no less than 111 saloons, not because the people wanted or patronized them to any great extent, but because saloons were needed for revenue, so it was claimed. . . .

And while this was in no way a typical American community, neither did it resemble Italy. No one with the least amount of Italian pride in him would want to boast that this was in any sense an Italian community. In fact, more than one investigator from Italy had pronounced it the very contradiction of all that Italian society stood for. . . . For in this city within a city it was the misfits of Italian society who were "i prominenti" and held dominance; it was those who could "bluff it through," who were the "bankers" and the publicists; it was the unscrupulous politician who controlled things; it was the quack who made his money; the shyster lawyer who held the people within the palm of his hand. . . . Again, here were thrown together by the hand of fate the humblest elements of Italian society, who though leading a peaceful existence, still were representing and perpetuating in a miniature way the interests of a hundred petty little principalities and powers in the limits of a single community. Here a thousand trifling, provincial and local animosities and controversies were brought together and fostered in a way that out-Babeled Babel. This conglomeration of folks would have been as much an anomaly in Italy as it was in America. The best of all that Italy stood for was not here. . . .

. . . Even with the small children, there are almost unconquerable difficulties to surmount as long as they are born or brought up in immigrant communities such as I have described. Can we really ever effect their assimilation so long as they live in these strange little worlds? . . .

A woman in our constituency had three children, two boys, one seven and the other five years old, and a baby girl. She was a widow and was having a bitter struggle to eke out an existence. She came to me one day requesting that I interest myself in placing the little girl in a nursery, and the boys in a kindergarten or school. I proceeded to make such arrangements at the public school, when one day she came to my office and broke out crying. I could not make out what the trouble was. After she calmed down, I asked her to tell me the difficulty. After evading several questions, she finally said: "Please don't send my children to an *American school,* for as soon as they learn English they will not be my children any more. I know many children who as soon as they learn English become estranged from their parents. I want to send my babies to a school where they can be taught in the Italian language". . . . And even though we stifle our emotions as we see a mother plead for the privilege of keeping her children always hers, we still must consider how we can manage to bring them into a knowledge and appropriation of American life and thought in the face of such an attitude.

CONSTANTINE M. PANUNZIO
The Soul of an Immigrant, 1969

Awaiting clearance at Castle Garden

THE TWENTIETH CENTURY

The early years of Hitler's rise to power precipitated the exodus to America of thousands of middle- and upper-class Jewish professionals. The uniquely painful assimilation of such refugee intellectuals is described by Martin Gumpert, an émigré physician and writer.

We have been preceded by millions, disappointed and hunted, rebellious and hungry for joy. They settled the coasts, drove their axes into the forests, navigated the streams, plowed the fields, founded cities and States, created liberty and power for themselves. . . .

We came late. We came laden with all the distress of a lost battle, with much doubt and false arrogance, with much useless and foolish ballast we valued even in the discard, with nothing but our naked life. Ignorant of the language and the country, penniless and presumptuous, we arrived with our needs and claims in America's moment of crisis. We thought we had much to give and soon saw ourselves more helpless than beggars, because we are not used to begging. . . .

. . . We are difficult arrivals. We do not know how to till the soil, we are no fellers of trees, and only a few of us are masters of a craft. We shelter libraries and phonograph records in our much too narrow rooms, and we cling fondly to the pleasures and arts amid which we have grown up. With every fiber we are still tied to the tragedy beneath which Europe is collapsing. . . .

What does one take along when one emigrates? In 1936 we still had our choice. There was a rumor that rooms over here were very small and wardrobes unnecessary. It takes a curious brand of heroism to surrender one's house furnishings voluntarily. One does not believe that it is possible to live on without one's books. The high transport charges could be paid in marks that would lose their value in any event as soon as one had left the country. . . . So long as the furniture trailed behind, there was a certain guarantee that one would not be completely at the mercy of the foreign land's barbarism, that the memories frozen into the pieces would not be wholly lost. . . .

Of course it feels good to have taken along shirts and suits and ties. Their cut may long keep the alien seal on the immigrant, but they relieve him of much worry. It is easy to change one's residence, but not one's appearance and one's everyday clothes. That external transformation can proceed but slowly. When the socks begin to show holes, when the first pair of shoes is bought, the first new hat acquired — these are way-stations in a mysterious metamorphosis that penetrates into every pore of one's being — until at last, after a long period of contemplation and readjustment, one makes up one's mind to buy an American tie. He who can manage to wear an American tie is a citizen beyond doubt.

For the workaday man the miracle of America begins not with the Statue of Liberty but with the shirts, that have much shorter tails here than in Europe, and with the shoes, that are not placed outside the hotel door at night. . . .

Emigration represents a break and an impact fortunately realized by but a few. In the middle-class sense it represents a bankruptcy, a degradation; unless one happens to be an Einstein, one is deprived of all one's marks of rank and left only with the opportunity to regain them under completely changed circumstances. To adventurers this offers a tremendous fascination, the chance of their lifetime. But we are not adventurers; we are doctors and businessmen with readily checked inventories. . . .

. . . [Emigration] is not merely a matter of fighting against time but also against space. For space alters time concepts — not solely in a tangible realistic way. Journeying from Europe to New York, one has to set one's watch every day, and between Berlin and California a time chasm of ten hours has to be bridged. And there is more. The mail takes longer; the distance from home to the baker's is longer; twilight is shorter; the seasons have different durations. Population masses are arranged differently; the land is administered and provisioned under completely changed conditions; the growth of cities and countryside follows the stroke of another clock. America changes the sense of time. . . .

All this is not merely on the surface. A different system rules the work-day — a different regulation of work and leisure; one finds oneself caught up in an utterly different biological circuit. And it is precisely these things of which the ingenuous immigrant hardly grows aware that become of the greatest importance for his ability to adapt himself. It is not a matter of technical details but of hearts beating in a different rhythm. Patience, will-power and flexibility are necessary to adapt to the new metabolism cells that had begun to harden in Europe. . . .

The situation of the immigrant who has had the misfortune of learning no English in school but only Latin and Greek is pathetic. He arrives in New York deaf and mute. The state into which he is translated is truly undignified and pathological.

To a man on an advanced intellectual level, loss of language is an almost insuperable shock. Waiters and children are able to gratify their speech functions with a small vocabulary. But to anyone who cares to translate subtle thoughts and desires into reasonable speech, who has a sense of responsibility for language, the infantile state into which he is forced is rather humiliating.

For a long time one is excluded from all discussion by the knowledge that one's speech is sheer torture to the ears of educated people and by the sorry privilege of having everything one says misunderstood. This long and painful process of rehabilitation, this rebirth of the power of speech extending over a period of decades, if indeed it is ever achieved, is unquestionably one of the severest trials of emigration. . . .

. . . Europe is unforgettable. I am deeply moved whenever I think of the pine-trees and the calm, gloomy lakes of my native Brandenburg. My reminiscent eyes delight in the vision of its hundred towns with their fine old walls, their splendid decay. And stacked here in my room are the volumes full of wisdom and art that gave content and direction to my childhood and to my youth.

But I knew when I left Germany that it was for good. And I know it even better today, five years later. In Aachen, on the border, I flashed the ten-mark note I was allowed to take along. I did not look back. It was a journey out of a realm of shadow. All my gratitude and all my love and tenderness and yearning for my lost homeland I took with me into the beckoning freedom and space of a new world. Pale and leaden the sky hung over Germany and the smoke-stacks of the factories vanished into the mist. . . .

There are many among us émigrés who cannot bear the freedom of this country — neither its intellectual freedom nor even less its physical freedom. Every European suffers from a prison psychosis. Freedom makes us melancholy and insecure. So greatly did we long for the utopian place of freedom that now that we can no longer escape anywhere — because we have escaped — now we look about anxiously for the bars to our cage. . . .

Freedom is no paradise. It is filled with danger, and without aim or order it becomes chaotic anarchy. There is much chaos in America at this time. The land is not yet weighed down with the ties and experiences to which the old world owed its pseudo-security. This land of abundance still lacks many of the institutions which the impact of progress created over there. . . .

We, the émigrés, have arrived here in the hour of decision. We have our own urgent, wretched problems. We must earn our bread, learn the language, understand our environment. True, the longing and sadness in our breast are understandable. Our arrogance is not. We are, after all, rescued fugitives. We stand in an awakening world that heretofore was strange and closed to us. We have the good fortune to stand by the side of our friends instead of bearing the yoke of our enemies. Our place is here. We must today begin to build the roof that shall be our indestructible shield for the future. We must make greater sacrifices, must be bolder and more steadfast than our new neighbors. Only then can we salvage our past as Europeans.

MARTIN GUMPERT
First Papers, 1941

Dedication-day festivities in the harbor honor the lady with a lamp

After traveling from Fascist Italy to Stockholm to receive the Nobel Prize in physics, Enrico Fermi determined to settle with his family in America. His wife, Laura, whose Jewish ancestry made their flight imperative, was acutely aware of the problems of adapting to an alien culture.

Wake up and dress. We have almost arrived. The children are already on deck."

In reluctant obedience to Enrico's peremptory voice, I emerged out of sleep and the warm comfort of my berth. It was the morning of January 2, 1939, and the "Franconia" was rolling placidly, with no hurry or emotion, bringing to its end a calm voyage.

On deck Nella and Giulio rushed to me, away from the watchful presence of their nurse.

"Land," Nella shouted; and Giulio extended a chubby finger in the direction of the ship's bow and repeated: "Land!"

Soon the New York skyline appeared in the gray sky, dim at first, then sharply jagged, and the Statue of Liberty moved toward us, a cold, huge woman of marble [copper], who had no message yet to give me.

But Enrico said, as a smile lit his face tanned by the sea:

"We have founded the American branch of the Fermi family."

I turned my eyes down to examine my children. They seemed more thoroughly scrubbed and polished than children I had seen in America [on a previous visit]. Their tailor-made coats and light-gray leggings were different from those of other children on the boat. On their curly heads the leather helmets we had bought in Denmark against the first northern rigors appeared alien. I looked at Enrico and at his markedly Mediterranean features, in which I could read the pride and the relief of one who has satisfactorily guided his expedition across land and sea, bearing all the responsibilities on his broad shoulders with an imperturbability that would have long been thrown off had it not been so deeply rooted in him. And I looked at the maid who had come along with us, . . . who could talk to none but us because she knew no English at all.

"This is no American family," I thought to myself. "Not yet". . . .

In the process of Americanization . . . there is more than learning language and customs and setting one's self to do whatever Americans can do. There is more than understanding the living institutions, the pattern of schools, the social and political trends. There is the absorbing of the background. The ability to evoke visions of covered wagons, to see the clouds of dust behind them in the golden deserts of the West, to hear the sound of thumping hoofs and jolting wheels over a mountain pass. The power to relive a miner's excitement in his boom town in Colorado and to understand his thoughts when, fifty years later, old and spare, but straight, no longer a miner, but a philosopher, he lets his gaze float along with the smoke from his pipe over the ghostlike remnants of his town. The acceptance of New England pride, and the participation in the long suffering of the South.

And there is the switch of heroes.

Suppose that *you* go to live in a foreign country and that this country is Italy. And suppose you are talking to a cultivated Italian, who may say to you:

"Shakespeare? Pretty good, isn't he? There are Italian translations of Shakespeare, and some people read them. As for myself, I can read English and have read some of Lamb's *Tales from Shakespeare*; the dream in midsummer; Hamlet, the neurotic who could not make up his mind; and *Romeo* and *Giulietta*. Kind of queer ideas you Anglo-Saxons have about Italians! Anyhow, as I was saying, Shakespeare is pretty good. But all those historical figures he brings in . . . not the most important ones. . . . We have to look up history books to follow him.

"Now you take Dante. *Here* is a great poet for you! A universal poet! Such a superhuman conception of the universe! Such visions of the upper and nether worlds! The church is still walking in Dante's steps after more than six centuries. And his history! He has made history alive. Read Dante and you know history. . . ."

In your hero worship there is no place for both Shakespeare and Dante, and you must take your choice. If you are to live in Italy and be like other people, forget Shakespeare. Make a bonfire and sacrifice him, together with all American heroes, with Washington and Lincoln, Longfellow and Emerson, Bell and the Wright brothers. In the shadow of that cherry tree that Washington chopped down let an Italian warrior rest, and let him be a warrior with a blond beard and a red shirt. A warrior who on a white stallion, followed by a flamboyant handful of red-shirted youths, galloped and fought the length of the Italian peninsula to win it for a king, a warrior whose name is Garibaldi. Let Mazzini and Cavour replace Jefferson and Adams, Carducci and Manzoni take the place of Longfellow and Emerson. Learn that a population can be aroused not only by Paul Revere's night ride but also by the stone thrown by a little boy named Balilla. Forget that a telephone is a Bell telephone and accept Meucci as its inventor, and remember that the first idea of an airplane was Leonardo's. Once you have made these adjustments in your mind, you have become Italianized, perhaps. Perhaps you have not and never will.

LAURA FERMI
Atoms in the Family, 1954

Liberty welcomes the homeless

Since the 1940's Puerto Ricans have emigrated to the United States in increasing numbers, settling in urban ghettos vacated by earlier immigrants. The effect of the "culture of poverty" on men such as Simplicio Ríos — a young Puerto Rican whom Oscar Lewis interviewed for his monumental study La Vida *— constitutes a profound challenge to the future of the land of liberty.*

We Puerto Ricans here in New York turn to each other for friendship. We go out on Fridays because that's the beginning of the *weekend*. A whole bunch of us Puerto Ricans go out together. Because as far as having friends of other races goes, the only one I have now is an American Negro who owns *un bar*.

Lots of people here have relatives in New Jersey, Pennsylvania, well, all over. So they often spend the *weekends* out of town. Others go to dances or to the beach. That's what we mostly do for entertainment in summer, have picnics at Coney Island. A big group of us Latins go together. Coney Island is full of people — all sorts mixed together. There you find white and black Americans. But many other beaches are different; they don't want Negroes or Puerto Ricans. . . .

I would like to work for the equality of Negroes and whites although I can't say that racial prejudice has really screwed me up much. But I don't agree with this business of the Negroes fighting. . . . I wouldn't get mixed up in those fights; they are Americans and understand each other. I'd let myself be drawn into something like that only if it was the Puerto Ricans who were in it. We have nothing to do with this business, so there's no need to get involved in fights.

If it were in my power to help the Puerto Ricans any way I chose, I would choose a good education for them, for the little ones who are growing up now. I would like them to have good schools where they would be taught English, yes, but Spanish too. That's what's wrong with the system up here — they don't teach Spanish to our children. That's bad, because if a child of yours is born and brought up here and then goes back to Puerto Rico, he can't get a job. How can he, when he knows no Spanish? It's good to know English. But Spanish is for speaking to your own people. That's the problem the children of Puerto Ricans have up here. They understand Spanish but they can't speak or write it.

A good education would help them to get jobs. Because sometimes Puerto Ricans come here to get a job and they can't find one. They want to work and earn money but don't have any schooling at all. They find themselves in a tight spot and maybe they have school children to support, so they'll accept any job that comes their way, usually the worst ones. That's one cause for the delinquency there is among us.

Another thing I would like to work for is better housing. Puerto Ricans can't get good apartments here because the landlords begin raising the rent. They don't want us because they say we're dirty and messy. All pay for what a few of us do. What happens is that when a Puerto Rican rents a place he cracks the plaster on the walls by driving in nails to hang pictures. And then he paints the different rooms different colors. Americans don't like that. So if a Puerto Rican goes to look for an apartment in a pretty part of the city, he finds they charge a hundred and fifty or two hundred dollars' rent. How can we pay that? A Puerto Rican here barely earns enough to pay for rent and food.

It's easy enough for married couples without children to get apartments, but a family with three or four children has trouble. Nobody wants to rent to them. And we Puerto Ricans usually do have children. So we have to look for months and then settle for the worst, for apartments full of rats and crawling with cockroaches. The more you clean, the more they come. There are more rats than people in New York, where we Latins live, I mean. . . .

When they see the way we live here, many Americans get the idea that we came over like the Italians and the Jews did. They have to come with a passport, see? They think we are the same. That and their racial prejudice are the things that make me dislike Americans. Whites here are full of prejudice against Latins and Negroes. In Puerto Rico it isn't like that. You can go any place a white man can, as long as you can pay your way. And a white man can sit down to eat at the same table as a Negro. But not here. That's why the United States is having so many troubles. That's why I say I don't like Americans. What I like is their country. The life here, the way, the manner of living.

SIMPLICIO RÍOS
Interview by Oscar Lewis, 1965

"THE NEW COLOSSUS"

Less than one hundred years ago Emma Lazarus wrote "The New Colossus" as a tribute to the Statue of Liberty. Since then her poem has become so well known that many Americans can recite the last lines from memory.

Not like the brazen giant of Greek fame,
With conquering limbs astride from land to land;
Here at our sea-washed, sunset gates shall stand
A mighty woman with a torch, whose flame
Is the imprisoned lightning, and her name
Mother of Exiles. From her beacon-hand
Glows world-wide welcome; her mild eyes command
The air-bridged harbor that twin cities frame.
"Keep, ancient lands, your storied pomp!" cries she
With silent lips. "Give me your tired, your poor,
Your huddled masses yearning to breathe free,
The wretched refuse of your teeming shore.
Send these, the homeless, tempest-tost to me,
I lift my lamp beside the golden door!"

EMMA LAZARUS
"The New Colossus," 1883

REFERENCE

Chronology of Immigration

Entries in boldface refer to the Statue of Liberty.

1607	Jamestown colony founded
1619	First Negro slaves reach Jamestown
1620	Voyage of the *Mayflower*
1630–40	Puritans emigrate to Massachusetts Bay Colony
1642	English Civil War radically decreases Puritan emigration
1654	First Jewish immigrants arrive in New Amsterdam
1683	Germans emigrate to Pennsylvania
1685	Revocation of Edict of Nantes increases French Huguenot emigration
1697	Slave trade expands as Royal African Company's monopoly ends
1707	Act of Union between Scotland and England increases Scottish emigration
1709	Major exodus from German Palatinate
1717	Parliament legalizes transportation of felons to colonies
1718	Major Scotch-Irish emigration begins
1733	Founding of Georgia, last of the original thirteen colonies
1740	Parliament grants British citizenship to alien colonists
1771–73	Agrarian crisis increases Scotch-Irish emigration
1775–83	American Revolution
1776	Declaration of Independence adopted
1783	Immigration resumes with Treaty of Paris
1787	U.S. Constitution drafted
1803	British Passenger Act limits numbers carried by emigrant ships
1807	Importation of Negro slaves prohibited
1815	First major wave of immigration begins — 5,000,000 arrive by 1860
1825	Britain repeals prohibition on emigration
1840	Founding of Cunard Line ushers in era of steamship passage
1845	Native American Party founded
1846–48	Potato famine causes major Irish peasant emigration
1848	German political refugees emigrate; gold discovered in California
1855	Castle Garden immigrant depot opened
1856	Know-Nothing Party collapses
1861–65	American Civil War
1863	Emancipation Proclamation issued
1865	Thirteenth Amendment prohibits slavery
1865	**Edouard de Laboulaye proposes memorial to Franco-American friendship**
1871	**Auguste Bartholdi conceives idea for Statue of Liberty in New York harbor**
1875	**Franco-American Union, French sponsor of statue, organized in Paris; Bartholdi completes first plaster model**
1876	**Forearm and torch of statue displayed at Philadelphia Centennial Exhibition**
1877	**American committee for construction of pedestal formed; Bedloe's Island designated as statue site**
1878	**Head of statue exhibited at Paris Exposition**
1881	**Franco-American Union raises necessary funds for statue's construction**
1882	Immigration law bars entry of lunatics, convicts, and those likely to become public charges; Chinese Exclusion Act bars immigration for ten years; Russian anti-Semitism increases Jewish emigration
1883	**Ground broken for construction of pedestal; Emma Lazarus writes "The New Colossus" for pedestal fund**
1884	**Statue presented to U.S. at Paris ceremony; cornerstone of pedestal laid**
1885	**New York *World* successfully raises $100,000 for pedestal; statue, in crates, arrives in New York harbor**

1886	**Official dedication ceremonies held**	1931	**Modernized floodlighting installed**
1891	Health qualifications set for immigrants; Russian pogroms spur Jewish emigration	1932	Immigrant processing ends at Ellis Island
1892	Ellis Island replaces Castle Garden as immigrant processing center	**1933**	**Statue placed under jurisdiction of National Park Service**
1894	Immigration Restriction League formed	1933	Rise of Nazism; emigration of Jewish and political refugees begins
1894–96	Moslem massacres of Armenian Christians lead to massive emigration	1933–36	New Deal social legislation enacted
1897	President Cleveland vetoes literacy tests for immigrants	1934	Philippine Independence Act restricts Filipino emigration
1901	**Statue placed under jurisdiction of War Department**	**1936**	**Statue's fiftieth anniversary honored at rededication ceremonies**
1903	**Emma Lazarus's poem placed on tablet affixed to pedestal of statue**	1941	U.S. enters World War II
1903	Anarchists and revolutionaries denied entry after assassination of McKinley	1942	Japanese-Americans evacuated from West Coast to detention camps
1904	Auguste Bartholdi dies	1945	Puerto Rican emigration increases
1905	Japanese/Korean Exclusion League formed	1946	War Brides Act admits foreign-born wives of servicemen
1907–8	Gentleman's Agreement with Japan limits immigration	1948	Displaced Persons Act admits 400,000 European refugees in four-year period
1913	California bars Japanese from owning land; President Taft vetoes literacy test for immigrants	1952	McCarran-Walter Act stiffens quotas
		1954	Ellis Island formally closed
1916	**Floodlighting system installed**	1956	Hungarian Revolution; Refugee Relief Act admits some 5,000 refugees
1917	Literacy test adopted over President Wilson's second veto; war declared on Germany	**1956**	**Bedloe's Island renamed Liberty Island; plans announced for an American Museum of Immigration at base of statue**
1919	Treaty of Versailles; alien radicals deported in big Red scare	1957	Special legislation admits additional Hungarian refugees
1921	Emergency law introduces restrictive quota system	1960	Emigration of Cuban refugees begins
1923	Ku Klux Klan reaches peak strength	1962	Legislation admits Hong Kong refugees
1924	**Statue declared a national monument**	1963	President Kennedy urges elimination of national origins quota system
1924	National Origins Act sets ceiling on immigration and establishes national origins quota system	**1965**	**Ellis Island declared part of statue national monument; conspiracy discovered to blow up statue and other monuments**
1929	Stock Market crashes; national origins quotas become operative	1965	Liberalized immigration legislation abolishes national origins quotas

Colossal Statues Through the Ages

Guarding the approaches to New York harbor is America's most famous lady, the statue of *Liberty Enlightening the World.* Designed as a memorial to Franco-American friendship, it has become a symbol of liberty to countless immigrants and native-born Americans.

Although the statue's French sponsor, the Franco-American Union, hoped to have the monument completed for the centennial celebration of American independence in 1876, financing and other difficulties delayed the official dedication until 1886. The $400,000 needed to cover construction costs was raised in France entirely by private subscription. American involvement was limited to providing the pedestal — and without an eleventh-hour fund-raising campaign by Joseph Pulitzer's New York *World,* it might not have been erected.

Auguste Bartholdi, the Alsatian sculptor who was commissioned to create the statue, conceived of Liberty as a majestic woman with placid features, draped in the sweeping curves of a Roman toga. Holding the burning torch of freedom in her right hand and cradling a tablet inscribed "July IV, MDCCLXXVI," in her left arm, she steps forward from the broken shackles of tyranny that lie at her bare feet.

The statue's dimensions are truly colossal: from her toes to her 7-spiked crown, she stands 151 feet high. Raised on a 65-foot base and an 89-foot granite pedestal, the mammoth figure towers just over 305 feet above the water. Her waist is 35 feet thick, her mouth 3 feet wide, her index finger 8 feet long, and each eye is 2½ feet wide.

Construction of the statue was a prodigious feat that required great in-genuity. The fact that funds were limited and that the completed figure would have to be transported across the ocean made the choice of material a crucial consideration. Bartholdi ultimately decided to construct a hollow figure consisting of thin sheets of hammered copper supported by a structural steel framework. The sculptor's four-foot-high working model was reproduced to one-fourth the final size. The figure was then enlarged, section by section. Carpenters made exact wooden patterns of each portion, onto which artisans hand-welded the 3/32-inch-thick copper plates. The intricate iron and steel skeleton, supported by four stout pylons, was painstakingly engineered by Gustave Eiffel to withstand the strongest buffeting by winds in the harbor.

The statue was formally presented to the U.S. Minister to France on July 4, 1884. The next year it was dismantled and packed in wooden crates, each piece carefully numbered, for the ocean voyage aboard the *Isère.* In late spring of 1885 the French warship reached Bedloe's Island, 1⅝ miles off the southern tip of Manhattan — the site designated by Congress. Before the War of 1812 a military base had been constructed on the twelve-acre island, and the statue was erected in the center of that abandoned, star-shaped fort.

Each year more than 1,000,000 visitors from all over the world flock to the island (since renamed Liberty Island), and many climb the 168-step spiral staircase to the observation balcony below the statue's crown for a magnificent view of the harbor and skyline of Manhattan. Lest tourists forget the statue's symbolic significance, a new American

Bartholdi's sketch of Liberty

Museum of Immigration has been planned for the base of the monument. Already on display are interim exhibits that describe the story of the statue and dramatize the epic role that immigrants have played in shaping America.

After returning to France following the dedication ceremonies for the Statue of Liberty, Bartholdi commented that he had "no doubt that with care and looking after the monument will last as long as those built by the Egyptians." The sculptor had toured Egypt in 1856 and again in 1868 and had been inspired by the grandeur of the immense monuments. He was particularly dazzled by the *Sphinx of Giza* — the legendary half-man, half-lion built about 2550 B.C. by the Fourth Dynasty pharaoh Chephren as part of his pyramid complex.

The enormous crouching figure was shaped from a knoll of soft limestone that had served as a quarry when the Great Pyramid of Chephren's predecessor Cheops was erected nearby. More than 240 feet long and 66 feet high, the Sphinx has been seriously eroded by the encroaching sands of the desert.

The face of the monument is an idealized portrait of the pharaoh Chephren, yet by the time of the New Kingdom the Sphinx had come to be worshiped as a god and was the center of a flourishing cult. During that period a young prince lay down for rest in the shadow of the Sphinx. In a dream, the statue promised to make him pharaoh of Egypt if he cleared away the sand and rubble that had half-buried the structure. The prince kept his end of the bargain — and within a few years he became the Eighteenth Dynasty ruler Tuthmosis IV. A large granite stele erected between the Sphinx's paws records the prophetic dream.

Despite the fact that its lion's mane is damaged, its eyes and nose are little more than holes, and its paws have been shored up with bricks and limestone blocks, the Sphinx is as awe-inspiring today as it must have been when it was built forty-five centuries ago. Although the ancient Greeks failed to list the Sphinx as one of the wonders of the world, they did include two other colossal statues — the *Olympian Zeus* and the *Colossus of Rhodes*.

The 40-foot-high gold and marble statue of the god Zeus seated on his throne was created by Phidias — regarded as the greatest of Greek sculptors — in the fifth century B.C. Lamentably, this masterpiece — along with a 40-foot-high statue of Athena that Phidias sculpted for the Parthenon — has been lost for centuries.

The Colossus of Rhodes was a bronze statue of the sun-god Helios designed by Chares of Lindus, a pupil of the famed Greek sculptor Lysippus. Reputed to have been over 100 feet high, it was commissioned to commemorate the successful defense of the island against the brutal year-long siege mounted by the Macedonian king Demetrius I in 305 B.C. According to tradition, the statue was cast from the bronze weapons and armor left behind by the retreating army.

Chares worked on the Colossus for twelve years before its official dedication in 280 B.C. The enormous figure was toppled by an earthquake in 224 B.C., and its metal fragments lay where they fell for nine hundred years before they were finally carted off and sold for scrap. An erroneous but persistent legend holds that the statue originally straddled the

The Sphinx of Giza

The Colossus of Rhodes

The statue of Nero

harbor and that ships passed between its outspread legs. In the twentieth century several civic-minded citizens of Rhodes have suggested that a modern replica of the statue be built. Since they propose to erect the Colossus in its fabled position astride the harbor (which would involve major technical difficulties) and since authorities dispute what the statue looked like, it is unlikely that the project will materialize.

The ancient Romans, no less than the Greeks, were expert at constructing larger-than-life-size figures. Statues of emperors, such as that of *Nero,* were the most common. After the fire of A.D. 64 had destroyed most of Rome, Nero ordered the construction of a 120-foot-high statue of himself, to be erected in the vestibule of his elaborate Golden House. The poet Martial described the figure as a "wondrous colossus . . . girt with rays," but only artists' conceptions of it remain. Some authorities think that the nearby Colosseum was named for Nero's statue.

The compelling appeal of colossal statues has continued unabated into the modern world. Countless oversized monuments have been erected in almost every nation to honor religious and temporal leaders, to commemorate significant events in a culture's history, and to memorialize abstract ideals.

In 1252 a monumental statue of Amida, a prominent Buddhist divinity, was cast by the sculptor Ono Goroemon at Kamakura, thirty-two miles from Tokyo. Today the *Kamakura Daibutsu,* or Great Buddha, sits serenely within the grounds of Kotokuin Temple. The large building that originally housed the figure was damaged by a storm in 1369, and a new structure built for it was washed away by

tidal waves in 1495; luckily the Buddha escaped from both incidents unscathed. The bronze monument, which weighs approximately 100 tons, is more than 40 feet high and has a circumference at the base of 96 feet. The diameter of each of the 656 curls on the statue's head is 9½ inches. Posed in the traditional meditative posture, with buttocks resting on heels, the Kamakura Buddha is a study in perfect repose and passionless calm. The position of the hands in the lap, with palms up and fingers touching, symbolizes the divinity's steadfast faith.

On a sharp rocky peak halfway across the world stands another monumental religious statue, *Christ the Redeemer.* The imposing concrete figure towers over Rio de Janiero from the top of Corcovado, or Hunchback Mountain, highest of the 365 peaks that dot the former capital of Brazil. The work of French sculptor Paul Landowski and Brazilian engineer Heitor da Silva Costa, it was dedicated in 1931. Christ is represented in the attitude of crucifixion — the span of his outstretched arms is 92 feet. The statue, weighing 1,145 tons and rising to an overall height of 125 feet, represents a triumph of artistic achievement and bold engineering.

On Uspallata Pass, high in the Andes on the Chilean-Argentinian border, a giant figure clasps a cross in his left hand and raises his right in benediction. Known as the *Christ of the Andes,* this famous religious statue was dedicated in 1904 to honor the peaceful settlement of border disputes between the two South American countries. The 14-ton, 26-foot-high monument is the work of Argentine artist Mateo Alonso.

Throughout history, victory in battle

The Kamakura Daibutsu

Christ the Redeemer

Michelangelo's David

The Iwo Jima memorial

has provided the subject matter for numerous colossal statues. During the Italian Renaissance, Michelangelo portrayed *David,* the youthful shepherd-king of the Old Testament, poised with a slingshot and calmly awaiting the approach of the giant Goliath. The heroic 17-foot figure, considered one of the world's greatest masterpieces, was carved from a single block of marble.

In the Teutoburger Forest in Lower Saxony a 56-foot statue, supported by a 95-foot arched base, commemorates the victory of the Germanic chieftain Arminius over the Roman general Varus in A.D. 9. The annihilation of its legions forced the Roman Empire to abandon plans for a province beyond the Rhine — with incalculable implications for the future of Europe. The huge statue, known as the *Hermanns-Denkmal,* was dedicated in 1875.

In this century, World War II inspired the creation of dozens of memorial statues. America's *Iwo Jima* monument in Washington was erected in 1954 and dedicated to the Marine dead of all U.S. wars. It depicts six Marines planting the flag atop Mount Suribachi on Iwo Jima, a Japanese island that was the scene of one of the Pacific front's most grueling battles. This unique bronze tableau — which precisely duplicates a contemporary news photograph — has an overall height of 75 feet, with each figure measuring approximately 32 feet high.

The tallest free-standing statue in the world, known as *Motherland,* commemorates the Soviet Red Army's victory at the battle of Stalingrad in 1942-43. The monument was dedicated in 1967 to honor the heroic resistance of the city (now Volgograd) against the unrelenting German siege. It consists of several small sculptures, an eternal flame, and an awesome 270-foot-high female figure with a sword clenched in her right hand.

At one time or another, almost every conceivable material has been employed to create colossal statues; perhaps the most startling recent trend is the use of United States mountain peaks.

On an area approximately the size of a football field, the mounted figures of three leaders of the ill-fated Confederacy — Jefferson Davis, Robert E. Lee, and Stonewall Jackson — have been carved into a Georgia mountain. Although the *Stone Mountain Confederate Memorial* was begun in the 1920's, production and financial difficulties soon halted progress. Work was resumed in 1963, when the state of Georgia purchased the site. Dedicated in 1970, the immense composition measures 190 feet by 305 feet.

An even larger monument is currently under construction in the Black Hills of South Dakota. In 1948 sculptor Korczak Ziolowski began work on an equestrian statue of *Chief Crazy Horse,* the martyred Sioux warrior who helped defeat General Custer in 1876. If completed, it will be the world's largest statue, with a projected height of 563 feet.

The most famous of these mountain-sculptures is *Mount Rushmore National Memorial,* on which the sculptor Gutzon Borglum carved the granite likenesses of four outstanding American presidents — Washington, Jefferson, Lincoln, and Theodore Roosevelt. The 60-foot-high busts are proportionate to a scale of men 465 feet tall. Completed in 1941, Mount Rushmore is a truly American monument, perhaps as symbolic of the nation's ideals as is the Statue of Liberty.

Motherland

Mount Rushmore National Memorial

Selected Bibliography

Bernard, William S., ed. *American Immigration Policy*. New York: Harper & Row, 1950.

Billington, Ray Allen. *The Protestant Crusade 1800-1860: A Study of the Origins of American Nativism*. New York: The Macmillan Co., 1938.

Boorstin, Daniel J. *The Americans: The Colonial Experience*. New York: Random House, 1958.

Brown, Francis James, ed. *One America*. Englewood Cliffs, N.J.: Prentice-Hall, 1952.

Cavanah, Frances, ed. *We Came to America*. Philadelphia: Macrae Smith Co., 1954.

Commager, Henry Steele, ed. *Immigration and American History*. Minneapolis: University of Minnesota Press, 1961.

Craven, Wesley. *The Legend of the Founding Fathers*. New York: New York University Press, 1956.

Ernst, Robert. *Immigrant Life in New York City: 1825-1863*. New York: Crown Press, 1949.

Fleming, Donald and Bailyn, Bernard, eds. *The Intellectual Migration: Europe and America, 1930-1960*. Cambridge: Harvard University Press, 1969.

Gschaedler, Andre. *True Light on the Statue of Liberty and Its Creator*. Narbeth, Pa.: Livingston Publishing Co., 1966.

Handlin, Oscar. *Boston Immigrants: A Study of Acculturation*, rev. ed. New York: Atheneum, 1968.

————. *Immigration as a Factor in American History*. Englewood Cliffs, N.J.: Prentice-Hall, 1959.

————. *The Americans*. Boston: Little, Brown and Co., 1963.

————. *The Uprooted*. Boston: Little, Brown and Co., 1951.

————, ed. *This Was America*. Cambridge: Harvard University Press, 1969.

Hansen, Marcus L., ed. *The Atlantic Migration, 1607-1860: A History of the Continuing Settlement of the United States*. New York: Harper & Row, 1961.

Higham, John. *Strangers in the Land: Patterns of American Nativism, 1860-1925*. New York: Atheneum, 1963.

Jones, Maldwyn A. *American Immigration*. Chicago: University of Chicago Press, 1960.

Kennedy, John F. *A Nation of Immigrants*. New York: Harper & Row, 1964.

Kent, Donald Peterson. *The Refugee Intellectual: The Americanization of the Immigrants*. New York: Columbia University Press, 1953.

Lewis, Oscar. *La Vida*. New York: Random House, 1965.

Maisel, Albert Q. *They All Chose America*. New York: Thomas Nelson and Sons, 1957.

Pauli, Herta and Ashton, E. B. *I Lift My Lamp: The Way of a Symbol*. New York: Appleton-Century-Crofts, 1948.

Rischin, Moses. *Promised City: New York's Jews, 1870-1914*. Cambridge: Harvard University Press, 1962.

Shannon, William. *The American Irish*. New York: The Macmillan Co., 1963.

Smith, James Morton. *Freedom's Fetters*. Ithaca: Cornell University Press, 1956.

Swanburg, W. A. *Pulitzer*. New York: Charles Scribner's Sons, 1967.

Wakefield, Dan. *Island in the City*. Boston: Houghton Mifflin Co., 1959.

Woodham-Smith, Cecil. *The Great Hunger*. New York: Harper & Row, 1963.

Acknowledgments and Picture Credits

The Editors make grateful acknowledgment for the use of excerpted material from the following works:

Atoms in the Family: My Life with Enrico Fermi by Laura Fermi. Copyright 1954 by Laura Fermi. The excerpt appearing on pages 157-58 is reproduced by permission of Laura Fermi and the University of Chicago Press.

First Papers by Martin Gumpert. Translated by Heinz and Ruth Norden. Copyright 1941 by Martin Gumpert. The excerpt appearing on pages 155-57 is reproduced by permission of Hawthorn Books, Inc.

Land of Their Choice: The Immigrants Write Home. Edited by Theodore C. Blegen. Copyright 1955 by University of Minnesota. The excerpts appearing on pages 140-42 are reproduced by permission of University of Minnesota Press.

La Vida by Oscar Lewis. Copyright 1965, 1966 by Oscar Lewis. The excerpt appearing on pages 159-60 is reproduced by permission of Random House, Inc. and Martin Secker & Warburg Limited.

The Americanization of Edward Bok by Edward Bok. Copyright 1920 by Charles Scribner's Sons. Copyright renewed 1948 by Mrs. Mary Louise Curtis Zimbalist. The excerpt appearing on page 152 is reproduced by permission of The American Foundation Incorporated.

The Promised Land by Mary Antin. Copyright 1940 by Mary Antin. The excerpt appearing on pages 148-50 is reproduced by permission of Houghton Mifflin Company.

The Soul of an Immigrant by Constantine M. Panunzio. Copyright 1969 by Arno Press Inc. The excerpts appearing on pages 150-51 and 153-54 are reproduced by permission of Arno Press Inc.

The Welsh in America. Edited by Alan Conway. Copyright 1961 by University of Minnesota. The excerpt appearing on page 146 is reproduced by permission of University of Minnesota Press.

The Editors would like to express their particular appreciation to John Veltri whose creative photographs of the Statue of Liberty and Ellis Island have made an invaluable addition to this book. In addition, the Editors would like to thank the following individuals and organizations for their assistance in producing this volume:

Mr. and Mrs. Joseph H. Hirshhorn, Greenwich, Connecticut
Mary-Jo Kline, New York
Kate Lewin, Paris
Musée Bartholdi, Colmar, France — Pierre Burger, Curator
Museum of the City of New York — Charlotte La Rue
National Committee for Employment of Youth — Margaret Toner
National Park Service — John W. Bond, Pasquale P. Buccolo, Robert F. Fenton, Louis Morris, Arthur L. Sullivan
The New-York Historical Society — Wilson Duprey
Mr. and Mrs. Germain Seligman, New York

The title or description of each picture appears after the page number (boldface), followed by its location. Photographic credits appear in parentheses.

ENDPAPERS Colored lithograph of Castle Garden after a painting by Andrew Melrose, *c.* 1887. Prints Division, New York Public Library HALF TITLE Symbol designed by Jay J. Smith Studio FRONTIS-PIECE (John Veltri) **9** China plate, France. 1885. Musée Bartholdi, Colmar (Russell Ash) **10-11** Photograph of New York harbor in the late 19th century. The New-York Historical Society **12** (John Veltri)

CHAPTER I **15** Wood engraving of Broadway at St. Paul's and Vesey Street, 1870's. The New-York Historical Society **16-17** Colored lithograph of *The Port of New York* by Currier and Ives, 1872. The New-York Historical Society **19** Photograph of Auguste Bartholdi. Musée Bartholdi, Colmar (Russell Ash) **20** top, Lion of Belfort; bottom, General Jean Rapp. Both by Auguste Bartholdi (Russell Ash) **21** Monument to those killed in the Franco-Prussian War by Auguste Bartholdi (Russell Ash) **23** Obverses of U.S. silver dollars for the years 1870, 1871, 1879. American Numismatic Society **24** left, Portrait of Charlotte Beysser by Ary Scheffer, 1855. Musée Bartholdi, Colmar (Russell Ash) **24** right, Detail from *Liberty Leading the People,* Eugène Delacroix, 1830. Louvre (Bulloz) **26-27** Six clay models of the Statue of Liberty by Auguste Bartholdi. Musée Bartholdi, Colmar (Russell Ash) **28** Watercolor sketch of the Statue of Liberty by Auguste Bartholdi. Musée Bartholdi, Colmar (Russell Ash) **30-31** *Le Pont Neuf* by Auguste Renoir, 1872. Collection Peter Benziger (Frank Lerner)

CHAPTER II **33** Bronze model of the head of the Statue of Liberty by Auguste Bartholdi. Museum of the City of New York **34** *The Burghers of Calais* by Auguste Rodin, 1886-87. The Joseph H. Hirshhorn Collection (John Veltri) **37** left, Photograph of Gustave Eiffel; right, Photograph of the partially erected Eiffel Tower. Both, Culver Pictures **38** top left, *Paris Through the Window* by Marc Chagall, 1913; top right, *The Eiffel Tower* by Pierre Delaunay, 1910. Both, The Solomon R. Guggenheim Museum **38** bottom, *The Pont de Grenelle and the Eiffel Tower* by Pierre Bonnard, 1912. Private Collection (Giraudon) **39** *The Eiffel Tower* by Georges Seurat, 1890. Collection Mr. and Mrs. Germain Seligman, New York **40** Photograph of Auguste Bartholdi in the Vavin Street Studio, Paris. Musée Bartholdi, Colmar (Russell Ash) **42-43** bottom, Photograph of the interior of the Paris workshop; **43** top, Photograph of the statue's left hand under construction. Both from Gontrand's *Album des Travaux de Construction de la Statue Colossale de la Liberté Destinée au Port de New-York,* Paris, 1883. Astor, Lenox & Tilden Foundations, New York Public Library **44-45** Two photographs of the progressive assemblage of the Statue of Liberty in the Paris workyard, from Gontrand's *Album des Travaux . . . ,* Paris, 1883. Astor, Lenox & Tilden Foundations, New York Public Library **46** Photograph of the Statue of Liberty near completion in the Paris workyard, from Gontrand's *Album des Travaux . . . ,* Paris, 1883 (Photo Hutin) **47** Photograph of the Statue of Liberty completed except for the torch in the Paris workyard, from Gontrand's *Album des Travaux . . . ,* Paris, 1883. Astor, Lenox & Tilden Foundations, New York Public Library **49** *Statue of Liberty on the Rue de Chazelles, Paris* by Victor Dargaud, 1884. Musée Carnavalet, Paris (Dorka)

CHAPTER III **51** Photograph of the arm and torch at the Philadelphia World's Fair, 1876. Collection Sirot, Paris **52** Obverse and reverse of commemorative Franco-American Union medal minted on October 28, 1886. Musée Bartholdi, Colmar (Russell Ash) **53** Photograph of William M. Evarts. The New-York Historical Society **54** Photograph of Joseph Pulitzer. The New-York Historical Society **55** Front page of *The World,* August 11, 1885. The New-York Historical Society **56** Photograph of the pedestal in 1883. National Park Service **57** Engraving of the *Isère* arriving in New York harbor, from *L'Illustration,* July 11, 1885. Museum of the City of New York **58** top, Engraving of the erection of the Statue of Liberty in New York harbor, from

Frank Leslie's Illustrated Newspaper, October 9, 1886. New York Public Library **58 bottom,** Engraving of workmen inside Liberty's head, from *Frank Leslie's Illustrated Newspaper,* October 23, 1886. Museum of the City of New York **59** *Unveiling of the Statue of Liberty* by Edward Moran, 1886. Museum of the City of New York **60-61** Photograph of the unveiling ceremony. Library of Congress **62** Deed offering the "Freedom of the City of New York" to Auguste Bartholdi, October 27, 1886. Musée Bartholdi, Colmar (Russell Ash) **63** Tiffany and Company testimonial presented to Auguste Bartholdi, November, 1886. Musée Bartholdi, Colmar (Russell Ash) **64 left,** Manuscript of "The New Colossus" by Emma Lazarus. Museum of the City of New York **64 right,** Engraving of Emma Lazarus, 1888. Picture Collection, New York Public Library **65** Engraving of the torch over New York harbor, from *Frank Leslie's Illustrated Newspaper,* June 20, 1885. New York Public Library **67** (John Veltri)

CHAPTER IV Sixteen impressionistic photographs of the Statue of Liberty, April 1970 (John Veltri)

CHAPTER V **85** Photograph of immigrants at Castle Garden, 19th century. Museum of the City of New York **86** Staffordshire soup plate showing Castle Garden, *c.* 1830. The New-York Historical Society **87** *The Battery, New York* by Samuel B. Waugh, 1855. Museum of the City of New York **88 top,** Photograph of immigrants on an Atlantic liner by Edwin Levick, December 10, 1906. Library of Congress **88 bottom,** Photograph of the steerage deck of the *S.S. Pennland* by Byron, 1893. The Byron Collection, Museum of the City of New York **89** Photograph of the deck of the *S.S. Amsterdam* by Frances Benjamin Johnston, 1910. Library of Congress **90-91** *Castle Garden* by Andrew Melrose, 1885. The New-York Historical Society **93** Photograph of immigrants on the Battery by Alice Austen, 1896. Picture Collection, New York Public Library **94 left,** *Outward Bound, the Quay of Dublin;* right, *Homeward Bound, the Quay of New York.* Both by J. Nicol and T. H. Maguire, May 24, 1854. The New-York Historical Society **95 top,** "Welcome to All," cartoon by Joseph Keppler, from *Puck,* April 28, 1880. The New-York Historical Society **95 bottom,** "Looking Backward," cartoon by Joseph Keppler, from *Puck,* January 11, 1893. Prints Division, New York Public Library **96** Photograph of Castle Garden by H. C. White Company, 1906. Library of Congress **98** details from "Liberty, How She Might Have Been," cartoon by Hy Meyer, from *Truth,* January 5, 1895. Picture Collection, New York Public Library **99** "Our Freedom Goddess — She Stands Fast and True," cartoon by C. J. Taylor, from *Puck,* October 27, 1886. New York Public Library

CHAPTER VI **101** Photograph of gypsy at Ellis Island. Picture Collection, New York Public Library **102** Photograph of paddle steamers at Ellis Island. Library of Congress **103** (John Veltri) **104 left,** Photograph of the Ellis Island Ferry. Picture Collection, New York Public Library **104 right,** Photograph of immigrants arriving at Ellis Island by Lewis Wickes Hine, 1926. George Eastman House **105 left,** Photograph of immigrants and officials at Ellis Island by Burt G. Phillips, 1907. Museum of the City of New York **105 right** (John Veltri) **106** Photograph of Russian immigrants at Ellis Island by Lewis Wickes Hine, 1905. George Eastman House **106-7** (John Veltri) **108** Photograph of immigrants in main hall at Ellis Island, Christmas, 1906. Library of Congress **109 top and bottom** (John Veltri) **110** Photograph of Slavic immigrants at Ellis Island by Lewis Wickes Hine, 1905. George Eastman House **111** (John Veltri) **112 left,** Photograph of female immigrants undergoing eye examination at Ellis Island, 1911; right, Photograph of male immigrants undergoing physical examination at Ellis Island, 1907. Both, Library of Congress **113 top and bottom** (John Veltri) **114** Photograph of immigrant in main hall at Ellis Island, *c.* 1910. Library of Congress **114-15** (John Veltri) **116** Photograph of German immigrants in dining hall at Ellis Island by Lewis Wickes Hine, *c.* 1926. George Eastman House **116-17 left and right** (John Veltri) **119** Photograph of immigrants on dock at Ellis Island, October 30, 1912. Library of Congress

CHAPTER VII **121** Photograph of Italian immigrants at Ellis Island by Lewis Wickes Hine, 1905. George Eastman House **122 top left,** Photograph of Finnish stowaway detained at Ellis Island, 1905; top middle, Photograph of a Russian steel worker at Homestead, Pennsylvania, 1909; top right, Photograph of a Czechoslovak immigrant at Ellis Island, 1926. All by Lewis Wickes Hine. George Eastman House **122 bottom,** Photograph of gypsies at Ellis Island. Picture Collection, New York Public Library **123 left,** Photograph of an Armenian Jew at Ellis Island, 1905; right, Photograph of a Russian Jewish woman at Ellis Island, 1905. Both by Lewis Wickes Hine. George Eastman House **124** (John Veltri) **126-27** Photograph of Orchard Street looking south from Hester Street by Byron, 1898. The Byron Collection, Museum of the City of New York **128 left,** Photograph of three basket sellers; right, Photograph of a paperboy. Both by Lewis Wickes Hine. National Committee for Employment of Youth **129 left and right,** Two photographs of women on Lower East Side by Lewis Wickes Hine. National Committee for Employment of Youth **130 top,** Photograph of family making artificial flowers by Lewis Wickes Hine. National Committee for Employment of Youth **130 bottom,** Photograph of a slum interior by Byron, 1896. The Byron Collection, Museum of the City of New York **131** Photograph of a Talmud school on Hester Street by Jacob A. Riis, 1889. The Jacob A. Riis Collection, Museum of the City of New York **132 top**

left, Photograph of a rear tenement on Roosevelt Street; top right, Photograph of a bathtub in an airshaft; bottom, Photograph of a street gang in Mullen's Alley. All by Jacob A. Riis. The Jacob A. Riis Collection, Museum of the City of New York   **133** Photograph of an Italian family in a Chicago tenement by Lewis Wickes Hine, 1910. George Eastman House   **135** (John Veltri)

IMMIGRANT MEMOIRS   **136** Photograph of immigrants looking toward New York City from the Ellis Island Pier, 1912. Library of Congress   **138** Engraving of the "Liberty Day" parade, from *Frank Leslie's Illustrated Newspaper*, November 6, 1886. New York Public Library   **142-43** Engraving of the interior of Castle Garden, from *Frank Leslie's Illustrated Newspaper*, December 29, 1855. The New-York Historical Society   **144-45** Engraving of a departing immigrant ship, from *Frank Leslie's Illustrated Newspaper*, January 12, 1856. The New-York Historical Society   **146-47** Engraving of the enlistment of Irish and German immigrants on the Battery, from *The Illustrated London News*, September 17, 1864. Museum of the City of New York   **148-49** Engraving of emigrants leaving Queenstown for New York, from *Harper's Weekly*, September 26, 1874. The New-York Historical Society   **152** Engraving of the vaccination of Russian and Polish emigrants, from *Frank Leslie's Illustrated Newspaper*, April 25, 1881. Library of Congress   **154-55** Engraving of a scene at Castle Garden, from *Harper's Weekly*, February 2, 1889. The New-York Historical Society   **156-57** Engraving of the illumination of New York harbor during the inauguration of the Statue of Liberty, from *The Illustrated London News*, November 20, 1886. New York Public Library   **158-59** Engraving of Jewish refugees from Russia passing the Statue of Liberty, from *Harper's Weekly*, 1892. New York Public Library

REFERENCE   **164** Sketch of the Statue of Liberty by Auguste Bartholdi. Musée Bartholdi, Colmar (Russell Ash)   **165** top, The Sphinx (The Rosicrucian Order)   **165** bottom, Engraving of the *Colossus of Rhodes*, from Joannes Gallaeus's *Speculum Diversarum Imaginum Speculativarum . . .*, Antwerp, 1638. Prints Division, New York Public Library   **166** top, An unknown artist's reconstruction of the statue of Nero (Fototeca Unione)   **166** center, *Kamakura Daibutsu* (Japan National Tourist Organization)   **166** bottom, *Christ the Redeemer* (Brazilian Government Trade Bureau)   **167** top, *David* by Michelangelo. Galleria dell'Accademia, Florence (Italian Government Travel Office)   **167** upper center, Marine Corps Iwo Jima Memorial (Defense Department)   **167** lower center, *Motherland* (Tass, from Sovfoto)   **167** bottom, Mount Rushmore (National Park Service)

Index

Andrew Melrose